Euphoria

Unleash Your Inner Joy and Achieve Enduring Happiness:
A Comprehensive Guide to Euphoria through Science-
Backed Strategies and Life-Changing Mindset Shifts in Self-
Help

Lance P. Richards

Euphoria: Unleash Your Inner Joy and Achieve Enduring Happiness: A Comprehensive Guide to Euphoria through Science-Backed Strategies and Life-Changing Mindset Shifts in Self-Help

Table of Contents

01: The Science of Euphoria: Understanding the Neurochemistry of Joy

Euphoria is a state of intense joy and pleasure that can transform our lives. Whether we experience it through love, work, hobbies, or other activities, euphoria has the power to uplift us, inspire us, and motivate us to achieve our goals. But what is the science behind euphoria? How does it work in our brains, and what can we do to cultivate more of it in our lives? In this chapter, we will explore the neurochemistry of joy and uncover the secrets to unlocking lasting euphoria through science-backed strategies and mindset shifts.

At the heart of euphoria is the brain's reward system, a complex network of neurons and neurotransmitters that regulate our feelings of pleasure and motivation. When we engage in activities that are pleasurable or rewarding, such as eating our favorite food, completing a challenging task, or experiencing a rush of adrenaline, the reward system is activated, releasing a surge of neurotransmitters such as dopamine, serotonin, and endorphins. These chemicals create a sense of pleasure and euphoria, reinforcing our behavior and motivating us to repeat it in the future.

But not all rewards are created equal, and some activities are more likely to trigger euphoria than others. For example, research has shown that activities that require effort and skill, such as playing a musical instrument or solving a complex problem, are more likely to trigger a surge of dopamine in the brain than activities that are passive or repetitive, such as watching TV or scrolling through social media. Similarly, social rewards, such as receiving praise or recognition from others, can also trigger a surge of dopamine and other feel-good chemicals in the brain, creating a sense of euphoria and motivation to continue the behavior.

So, if we want to cultivate more euphoria in our lives, we need to focus on activities that are challenging, rewarding, and meaningful. This might mean pursuing a hobby or skill that we are passionate about, setting ambitious goals for ourselves, or seeking out opportunities for social connection and recognition. By engaging in these activities, we can activate our brain's reward system and experience lasting feelings of joy and motivation.

But the science of euphoria goes beyond simply engaging in

rewarding activities. Our mindset and beliefs also play a crucial role in shaping our experiences of joy and pleasure. For example, research has shown that people who have a growth mindset, or a belief that their abilities can be developed through hard work and dedication, are more likely to experience euphoria and motivation than those with a fixed mindset, who believe that their abilities are predetermined and unchangeable.

Similarly, gratitude and positive thinking have been shown to enhance our experiences of joy and pleasure. When we focus on the positive aspects of our lives and express gratitude for the good things we have, we activate the brain's reward system and create a sense of well-being and euphoria. This might mean keeping a gratitude journal, practicing mindfulness, or simply taking time to appreciate the beauty and wonder of the world around us.

In addition to mindset and beliefs, our physical health and well-being also play a crucial role in our experiences of euphoria. Exercise, for example, has been shown to activate the brain's reward system and release feel-good chemicals such as endorphins, creating a sense of joy and motivation.

Similarly, getting enough sleep, eating a healthy diet, and managing stress can all enhance our experiences of euphoria and promote lasting happiness and well-being.

In conclusion, euphoria is a powerful state of joy and pleasure that can transform our lives. By understanding the science behind euphoria and cultivating science-backed strategies and mindset shifts, we can unlock lasting happiness and well-being, and unleash our inner joy for a more fulfilling life. So, whether we are pursuing our passions, setting ambitious goals, cultivating a positive mindset, or taking care of our physical health, let us embrace the power of euphoria and use it to propel us towards a more fulfilling and joyful life.

One important factor to consider when it comes to cultivating euphoria is the role of social connection. Research has shown that socializing and connecting with others can trigger a surge of dopamine in the brain, creating feelings of pleasure and euphoria. This might mean spending time with friends and family, joining a social club or group, or volunteering in our community. By fostering social connections, we can not only enhance our experiences of joy and pleasure but also improve our overall well-being and sense of purpose.

Another important factor to consider is the role of creativity and self-expression. Engaging in creative activities, such as art, music, or writing, has been shown to activate the brain's reward system and release dopamine, creating a sense of pleasure and euphoria. By tapping into our creative potential and expressing ourselves in meaningful ways, we can cultivate lasting happiness and fulfillment in our lives.

Finally, it is important to note that euphoria is not always a positive experience. In some cases, euphoria can be a symptom of a mental health condition such as mania or substance abuse. It is important to seek professional help if euphoria becomes excessive, interferes with daily functioning, or is accompanied by other symptoms such as anxiety, depression, or suicidal thoughts.

In summary, the science of euphoria reveals that joy and pleasure are not just fleeting experiences but powerful forces that can transform our lives. By understanding the role of the brain's reward system, cultivating science-backed strategies and mindset shifts, and embracing the power of social connection, creativity, and self-expression, we can unlock lasting happiness and well-being and achieve enduring euphoria in our lives. So, let us unleash our inner joy and pursue a life of meaning, purpose, and fulfillment, one euphoric moment at a time.

02: The Roadmap to Euphoria: Mapping Out Your Path to Happiness

The pursuit of happiness is an age-old quest that has eluded many throughout human history. Despite its intangibility, people have long sought ways to achieve a state of joy and contentment that lasts beyond fleeting moments. And while happiness is often portrayed as an elusive and mysterious concept, the truth is that it can be achieved through science-backed strategies and mindset shifts.

This chapter will guide you through the roadmap to euphoria, mapping out your path to happiness. By following the steps outlined here, you can unleash your inner joy and achieve enduring happiness.

Step 1: Understand the Science of Happiness

The first step to achieving euphoria is to understand the science of happiness. Research has shown that happiness is not a result of external circumstances, but rather an internal state of mind. While external factors such as wealth, health, and social status can certainly impact our happiness, they do not determine it.

02: THE ROADMAP TO EUPHORIA: MAPPING OUT YOUR PATH TO HAPPINESS

Instead, happiness is largely influenced by our thoughts, feelings, and behaviors. By cultivating positive thoughts, emotions, and actions, we can increase our levels of happiness and experience greater joy in our lives.

Step 2: Cultivate Positive Emotions

One of the most effective ways to increase our happiness is to cultivate positive emotions. Positive emotions such as gratitude, love, joy, and contentment can help us feel happier, more fulfilled, and more connected to the world around us.

To cultivate positive emotions, it's important to focus on the good things in our lives. This might involve practicing gratitude by keeping a gratitude journal, expressing appreciation to loved ones, or simply taking time to reflect on the blessings in our lives.

Other strategies for cultivating positive emotions include engaging in activities that bring us joy, such as hobbies, sports, or creative pursuits, and surrounding ourselves with positive people who lift us up and support our well-being.

Step 3: Develop a Growth Mindset

Another key factor in achieving euphoria is developing a growth mindset. A growth mindset is a belief system that emphasizes the power of effort, persistence, and learning in achieving our goals and fulfilling our potential.

People with a growth mindset tend to be more resilient, adaptable, and optimistic, which can help them overcome obstacles and pursue their dreams with greater confidence and determination.

To develop a growth mindset, it's important to embrace challenges and see them as opportunities for growth and learning. This might involve setting ambitious goals, seeking out new experiences, and seeking feedback from others to help us improve and grow.

Step 4: Practice Self-Care

Self-care is another critical component of achieving euphoria. Self-care involves taking care of our physical, emotional, and mental health, and making time for activities and practices that help us feel rejuvenated, refreshed, and renewed.

Self-care can take many forms, from getting enough sleep and exercise to engaging in relaxation techniques such as meditation, yoga, or deep breathing. It can also involve practicing self-compassion and self-acceptance, recognizing that we are all imperfect and deserving of love and kindness.

Step 5: Cultivate Meaningful Relationships

Finally, cultivating meaningful relationships is a crucial element of achieving euphoria. Humans are social creatures, and our relationships with others play a significant role in our happiness and well-being.

To cultivate meaningful relationships, it's important to prioritize our connections with others and invest time and energy in building and maintaining strong bonds. This might involve spending time with loved ones, joining social groups or clubs, or volunteering in our communities.

By cultivating positive emotions, developing a growth mindset, practicing self-care, and cultivating meaningful relationships, we can map out our path to euphoria and achieve enduring happiness. While the journey may not always be easy, the rewards of a joyful, fulfilling life are well worth the effort.

03: Breaking Free from Negative Thought Patterns: Overcoming Limiting Beliefs

Introduction

Negative thought patterns can be a major obstacle to experiencing euphoria and enduring happiness. These thought patterns are often rooted in limiting beliefs that we have internalized over time, which shape how we view ourselves, the world around us, and our place in it. These beliefs can be so ingrained that we don't even realize they're holding us back.

But it's possible to break free from these negative thought patterns and limiting beliefs. In this chapter, we'll explore some science-backed strategies and mindset shifts that can help you overcome negative thought patterns and cultivate a more positive and empowered mindset.

Understanding Limiting Beliefs

Before we can work on breaking free from negative thought patterns, it's important to understand what they are and how they develop. Limiting beliefs are essentially negative beliefs about ourselves or the world that we have internalized over time. They can stem from a variety of sources, including childhood experiences, cultural norms and expectations, and even media and advertising.

Some common limiting beliefs include:

– I'm not good enough

– I don't deserve happiness/success/love/etc.

– The world is a dangerous place

– People can't be trusted

– I'm not smart/talented/creative/etc. enough

These beliefs can be so deeply ingrained that we don't even realize we're holding onto them. They can shape our thoughts, emotions, and behaviors in subtle and insidious ways, leading us to feel stuck, helpless, and unfulfilled.

But the good news is that we can change these beliefs. It takes time and effort, but it's possible to break free from limiting beliefs and develop a more positive and empowering mindset.

Identifying Negative Thought Patterns

The first step in breaking free from negative thought patterns is to identify them. This can be challenging, as these patterns can be so ingrained that they feel like second nature. But with practice and self-awareness, it's possible to recognize when you're engaging in negative self-talk or cognitive distortions.

Some common negative thought patterns include:

– All-or-nothing thinking (e.g., "I either succeed completely or I'm a failure")

– Catastrophizing (e.g., "If I fail at this, my whole life is ruined")

– Discounting the positive (e.g., "Yeah, I got an A on that test, but it was easy")

– Personalizing (e.g., "He didn't call me back because he doesn't like me")

03: BREAKING FREE FROM NEGATIVE THOUGHT PATTERNS: OVERCOMING LIMITING BELIEFS

– Overgeneralizing (e.g., "I always mess things up")

When you catch yourself engaging in these negative thought patterns, try to pause and examine them objectively. Ask yourself if they're based in reality, or if they're distorted by your own biases and beliefs. Challenge them with more positive and realistic alternatives, and practice reframing your thoughts in a more empowering way.

Shifting Your Mindset

Breaking free from negative thought patterns requires more than just identifying and challenging them. It also involves cultivating a more positive and empowering mindset. This means adopting a growth mindset, which is the belief that our abilities and intelligence can be developed through dedication and hard work.

Some key elements of a growth mindset include:

– Embracing challenges as opportunities for growth

– Learning from failure and setbacks

– Cultivating a sense of curiosity and a love of learning

03: BREAKING FREE FROM NEGATIVE THOUGHT PATTERNS: OVERCOMING LIMITING BELIEFS

– Focusing on effort and persistence, rather than innate talent or intelligence

– Seeking out feedback and using it to improve

By adopting a growth mindset, we can break free from the limiting beliefs that hold us back and cultivate a more positive and empowered outlook on life.

Practicing Self-Compassion

Another important aspect of breaking free from negative thought patterns is practicing self-compassion. This means treating ourselves with kindness, understanding, and acceptance, even in the face of failure or difficulty.

Self-compassion involves three key elements:

– Self-kindness: Being warm and understanding towards ourselves when we suffer or fail, rather than harshly self-critical.

– Common humanity: Recognizing that suffering and difficulty are a normal part of the human experience, and that we're not alone in our struggles.

03: BREAKING FREE FROM NEGATIVE THOUGHT PATTERNS: OVERCOMING LIMITING BELIEFS

– Mindfulness: Being present and aware of our thoughts and emotions, without judgment or criticism.

By practicing self-compassion, we can break free from the negative self-talk and self-criticism that can hold us back and cultivate a greater sense of self-worth and resilience.

Developing Positive Habits

In addition to shifting our mindset and practicing self-compassion, developing positive habits can also be a powerful way to break free from negative thought patterns and cultivate lasting happiness and fulfillment.

Some key habits that can help promote a positive mindset and overall well-being include:

– Gratitude: Taking time each day to reflect on the things we're grateful for can help shift our focus away from negative thoughts and towards the positive aspects of our lives.

– Mindfulness: Practicing mindfulness meditation or simply being present and aware of our thoughts and emotions can help us become more attuned to our inner experiences and break free from negative thought patterns.

03: BREAKING FREE FROM NEGATIVE THOUGHT PATTERNS: OVERCOMING LIMITING BELIEFS

– Exercise: Regular physical activity has been shown to have numerous physical and mental health benefits, including reducing stress and anxiety and promoting feelings of well-being.

– Social connection: Building strong relationships and social support networks can help us feel more connected and fulfilled, and can provide a buffer against stress and adversity.

Conclusion

Breaking free from negative thought patterns and limiting beliefs is a key step towards experiencing euphoria and enduring happiness. By identifying and challenging negative thought patterns, adopting a growth mindset, practicing self-compassion, and developing positive habits, we can cultivate a more positive and empowering outlook on life.

Remember, changing deeply ingrained beliefs and thought patterns takes time and effort. Be patient and kind to yourself as you work towards developing a more positive and fulfilling way of thinking and being. With dedication and practice, you can break free from limiting beliefs and unlock

03: BREAKING FREE FROM NEGATIVE THOUGHT PATTERNS: OVERCOMING LIMITING BELIEFS

your full potential for joy and happiness.

04: Finding Meaning and Purpose: The Key to Lasting Fulfillment

As human beings, we all have a deep-seated desire to find meaning and purpose in our lives. It is a universal need that transcends age, gender, race, and culture. Without meaning and purpose, life can feel empty and unfulfilling, leaving us with a sense of aimlessness and despair.

In this chapter, we will explore the concept of meaning and purpose, and how it relates to lasting fulfillment and happiness. We will also discuss practical strategies and mindset shifts that can help you discover and cultivate your own sense of purpose and meaning in life.

What is Meaning and Purpose?

The terms "meaning" and "purpose" are often used interchangeably, but they refer to slightly different things. Meaning is the sense of significance or value that we attach to something, while purpose is the reason why something exists or is done. Together, they form a powerful combination that can provide us with a sense of direction and motivation in life.

04: FINDING MEANING AND PURPOSE: THE KEY TO LASTING FULFILLMENT

Finding meaning and purpose is a deeply personal journey that requires self-reflection, introspection, and a willingness to be vulnerable. It is not a one-size-fits-all approach, and what works for one person may not work for another. However, there are some common themes and strategies that can help guide you along the way.

The Importance of Meaning and Purpose

Research has shown that having a sense of meaning and purpose in life is associated with numerous benefits, including greater happiness, resilience, and longevity. It can also help us navigate difficult times and overcome challenges, as we are more likely to stay motivated and focused when we have a clear sense of why we are doing something.

Conversely, a lack of meaning and purpose can lead to feelings of apathy, boredom, and dissatisfaction. Without a clear sense of direction or motivation, we may feel stuck or unfulfilled, which can impact our mental and physical health.

So, how can we find meaning and purpose in life? Let's explore some practical strategies and mindset shifts that can help.

Strategy 1: Reflect on Your Values

Our values are the things that we hold dear and are important to us. They can include things like honesty, kindness, creativity, and adventure. Reflecting on your values can help you identify what is truly important to you and what gives your life meaning.

Take some time to think about what values resonate with you. You can make a list or create a vision board that represents your values. Once you have a clear sense of what matters to you, you can use these values as a guidepost for making decisions and setting goals.

Strategy 2: Explore Your Interests and Passions

Our interests and passions can give us a sense of purpose and fulfillment. When we engage in activities that we enjoy and feel passionate about, we are more likely to feel energized and motivated.

Take some time to explore your interests and passions. You can try new things or revisit old hobbies that you may have neglected. Ask yourself what activities bring you joy and make you feel alive. Once you have identified your interests and passions, find ways to incorporate them into your daily life.

Strategy 3: Set Meaningful Goals

Setting goals that are meaningful and aligned with our values and passions can give us a sense of purpose and direction. When we have a clear goal in mind, we are more likely to stay motivated and focused.

When setting goals, ask yourself what is truly important to you and what you want to achieve. Make sure that your goals are specific, measurable, and realistic. Also, make sure that your goals are aligned with your values and passions.

Strategy 4: Cultivate Gratitude

Gratitude is the practice of focusing on the good things in life and being thankful for them. Cultivating gratitude can help us find meaning and purpose in the present moment, and appreciate the things that we have in our lives.

One way to cultivate gratitude is to keep a gratitude journal.

Each day, write down three things that you are grateful for. They can be big or small things, such as a warm cup of coffee or a supportive friend. Taking the time to reflect on the good things in your life can help you develop a more positive outlook and appreciate the meaningful moments in your day-to-day life.

Strategy 5: Connect with Others

Human beings are social creatures, and we thrive on connection and community. Building meaningful relationships and connections with others can give us a sense of belonging and purpose.

Take the time to connect with others in meaningful ways. This can be through volunteering, joining a club or community organization, or simply reaching out to friends and family. Cultivating a sense of connection and community can help you find meaning and purpose in your interactions with others.

Mindset Shifts for Finding Meaning and Purpose

In addition to these practical strategies, there are also some mindset shifts that can help you find meaning and purpose in life.

Shift 1: Embrace Uncertainty

Life is full of uncertainty, and it can be easy to feel anxious or overwhelmed by the unknown. However, embracing uncertainty can help you find meaning and purpose in the present moment.

Instead of focusing on what may or may not happen in the future, try to focus on what you can do right now to create meaning and purpose in your life. Embrace the unknown and use it as an opportunity to explore new possibilities and take risks.

Shift 2: Focus on Growth

Finding meaning and purpose in life is not a one-time event. It is an ongoing process of growth and self-discovery.

Rather than focusing on achieving a specific goal or outcome, focus on the journey and the growth that comes with it. Celebrate your successes and learn from your failures. Use every experience as an opportunity to learn and grow.

04: FINDING MEANING AND PURPOSE: THE KEY TO LASTING FULFILLMENT

Shift 3: Be Present

Finding meaning and purpose in life requires being present in the moment and fully engaged in what you are doing.

Instead of worrying about the past or the future, try to focus on what you can do right now to create meaning and purpose in your life. Be fully engaged in your interactions with others, and take the time to appreciate the small moments of joy and happiness that come your way.

Conclusion

Finding meaning and purpose in life is a lifelong journey, and it requires a combination of practical strategies and mindset shifts. By reflecting on your values, exploring your interests and passions, setting meaningful goals, cultivating gratitude, and connecting with others, you can create a sense of purpose and direction in your life.

In addition, by embracing uncertainty, focusing on growth, and being present in the moment, you can develop a mindset that is conducive to finding meaning and purpose in all areas of your life.

04: FINDING MEANING AND PURPOSE: THE KEY TO LASTING FULFILLMENT

Remember, finding meaning and purpose is not a one-size-fits-all approach. It requires self-reflection, introspection, and a willingness to be vulnerable. However, with the right strategies and mindset shifts, you can unleash your inner joy and achieve enduring happiness through a life filled with meaning and purpose.

05: Building Resilience: Overcoming Adversity and Bouncing Back Stronger

Life is full of ups and downs, and it is the downs that often leave us feeling defeated, helpless, and hopeless. But what if there was a way to bounce back from adversity stronger and more resilient than ever before? That is the power of building resilience, and in this chapter, we will explore the science-backed strategies and mindset shifts that can help you overcome adversity and unleash your inner strength.

The first step in building resilience is to understand what it is and how it works. Resilience is the ability to adapt and recover in the face of adversity, trauma, or stress. It is not a fixed trait but rather a set of skills that can be developed and strengthened over time. Research shows that resilient individuals have better mental and physical health outcomes, higher levels of life satisfaction, and greater success in achieving their goals.

So how can you start building resilience in your own life? One of the most effective strategies is to cultivate a growth mindset. This means viewing challenges and setbacks as opportunities for learning and growth rather than as insurmountable obstacles. Research has shown that individuals with a growth mindset are more resilient and better able to bounce back from adversity.

Another key strategy is to practice self-care. This includes taking care of your physical, emotional, and mental health needs. Eating a healthy diet, getting regular exercise, and getting enough sleep are all important for building physical resilience. Engaging in activities that bring you joy, such as hobbies or spending time with loved ones, can help bolster emotional resilience. And practicing mindfulness, meditation, or other stress-reducing techniques can help build mental resilience.

Another important aspect of building resilience is developing a strong support network. Having a network of family, friends, and other supportive individuals can provide a sense of belonging and social connection that can help buffer the effects of stress and adversity. It is also important to seek out professional help if you are struggling with mental health issues such as depression or anxiety.

Another strategy for building resilience is to practice gratitude. Gratitude involves focusing on the positive aspects of your life and expressing appreciation for the good things that come your way. Research has shown that practicing gratitude can improve mental health outcomes, increase life satisfaction, and enhance resilience.

Finally, it is important to develop a sense of purpose and meaning in your life. This can involve setting goals and working towards achieving them, as well as finding ways to contribute to your community or make a positive impact in the world. Having a sense of purpose and meaning can help provide a sense of direction and motivation during difficult times.

In conclusion, building resilience is an important skill for navigating life's challenges and bouncing back stronger than ever before. By cultivating a growth mindset, practicing self-care, developing a strong support network, practicing gratitude, and finding a sense of purpose and meaning, you can become more resilient and better equipped to handle whatever life throws your way. Remember, resilience is not a fixed trait but rather a set of skills that can be developed and strengthened over time. So start building

05: BUILDING RESILIENCE: OVERCOMING ADVERSITY AND BOUNCING BACK STRONGER

your resilience today and unleash your inner strength and joy!

06: The Power of Gratitude: Cultivating Appreciation and Joy

The human brain is a remarkable machine capable of processing vast amounts of information in a fraction of a second. However, it is often programmed to focus on the negative aspects of life, leaving us feeling stressed, anxious, and unhappy. The good news is that the power of gratitude can help to shift our focus from the negative to the positive, leading to a more fulfilling and joyful life.

Gratitude is the act of being thankful and appreciative for the good things in our lives, whether big or small. It is a practice that has been used for centuries to cultivate inner peace, joy, and contentment. In recent years, science has begun to shed light on the power of gratitude, demonstrating its ability to improve mental and physical health, strengthen relationships, and increase overall well-being.

This chapter will explore the science behind gratitude and provide practical strategies for cultivating appreciation and joy in your life.

The Science of Gratitude

06: THE POWER OF GRATITUDE: CULTIVATING APPRECIATION AND JOY

Gratitude is a positive emotion that activates the reward center in the brain, releasing dopamine and serotonin, which are neurotransmitters associated with pleasure and contentment. When we experience gratitude, we are more likely to feel happy, optimistic, and satisfied with life.

Studies have shown that people who practice gratitude on a regular basis experience a wide range of benefits, including:

Improved Mental Health: Gratitude has been found to reduce symptoms of depression and anxiety, increase self-esteem, and enhance overall well-being.

Better Physical Health: Gratitude has been linked to improved immune function, lower blood pressure, and reduced inflammation, all of which contribute to better physical health.

Stronger Relationships: Gratitude can help to strengthen relationships by fostering feelings of closeness, trust, and appreciation.

Increased Resilience: Gratitude has been shown to improve resilience, helping individuals to cope with stress and adversity more effectively.

Cultivating Gratitude

Gratitude is not just an emotion; it is a practice that can be cultivated through daily habits and intentional mindset shifts. Here are some strategies for cultivating gratitude in your life:

Keep a Gratitude Journal: Taking time each day to write down three things you are grateful for can help to shift your focus from the negative to the positive. This practice can help you to develop a more positive outlook on life, leading to increased happiness and well-being.

Practice Mindfulness: Mindfulness is the practice of being fully present in the moment, without judgment or distraction. By practicing mindfulness, you can become more aware of the good things in your life and cultivate a sense of appreciation and gratitude.

Express Gratitude to Others: Taking time to express gratitude to the people in your life can help to strengthen relationships and foster feelings of connection and appreciation. This can be as simple as sending a thank-you note or expressing your gratitude in person.

Focus on Abundance: Instead of focusing on what you don't have, focus on the abundance in your life. This can be as simple as appreciating the beauty of nature, the love of family and friends, or the simple pleasures of life.

Practice Gratitude Meditation: Gratitude meditation involves focusing on the things you are grateful for and allowing those feelings to fill your body and mind. This practice can help to cultivate feelings of joy and contentment, leading to increased happiness and well-being.

Conclusion

The power of gratitude is a scientifically-backed strategy for cultivating joy, appreciation, and contentment in life. By practicing gratitude on a regular basis, we can shift our focus from the negative to the positive, leading to improved mental and physical health, stronger relationships, and increased overall well-being. So take some time today to appreciate the good things in your life, and watch as your inner joy and happiness begin to flourish.

07: Cultivating Mindfulness: Being Present and Finding Peace

Introduction

We all have a tendency to dwell in the past or worry about the future, but how often do we stop and appreciate the present moment? Mindfulness is the art of being present and fully engaged in the here and now, and it's a powerful tool for achieving lasting happiness and inner peace.

In this chapter, we'll explore the science behind mindfulness, the benefits it offers, and practical strategies for cultivating it in your daily life. By the end of this chapter, you'll have a deeper understanding of mindfulness and be equipped with the tools to start practicing it yourself.

The Science of Mindfulness

Mindfulness has been studied extensively in recent years, and the research shows that it offers a wide range of benefits for both mental and physical health. Studies have found that mindfulness can:

– Reduce symptoms of anxiety and depression

07: CULTIVATING MINDFULNESS: BEING PRESENT AND FINDING PEACE

– Improve mood and emotional regulation

– Increase resilience and coping skills

– Enhance attention and cognitive function

– Lower blood pressure and reduce chronic pain

– Boost the immune system

But how does mindfulness achieve all these benefits? The answer lies in the way it changes the brain.

Research has shown that mindfulness practice can lead to changes in the structure and function of the brain. Regular mindfulness practice has been found to increase activity in the prefrontal cortex, the part of the brain responsible for executive function, decision making, and emotional regulation. This increased activity in the prefrontal cortex has been linked to better emotional regulation and cognitive function.

At the same time, mindfulness practice has been found to decrease activity in the amygdala, the part of the brain responsible for the fight or flight response. This decreased activity in the amygdala has been linked to lower levels of stress and anxiety.

These changes in brain structure and function help to explain why mindfulness offers so many benefits for mental and physical health.

Practical Strategies for Cultivating Mindfulness

Now that we understand the science behind mindfulness, let's look at some practical strategies for cultivating mindfulness in your daily life.

Mindful Breathing

One of the easiest and most effective ways to practice mindfulness is through mindful breathing. To practice mindful breathing, simply sit comfortably with your eyes closed and focus on your breath. Pay attention to the sensation of the breath as it enters and leaves your body, and notice any thoughts or feelings that arise without judgment. If your mind wanders, simply bring your attention back to your breath.

You can practice mindful breathing for as little as a few

minutes a day, and it's a great way to start your day or take a quick break during a busy day.

Mindful Eating

Mindful eating is another powerful way to practice mindfulness. To practice mindful eating, choose a small amount of food, such as a piece of fruit or a small snack, and eat it slowly and deliberately. Pay attention to the flavors, textures, and sensations of the food as you eat it, and notice any thoughts or feelings that arise without judgment.

Practicing mindful eating can help you to develop a healthier relationship with food and reduce mindless eating habits.

Mindful Movement

Mindful movement, such as yoga or tai chi, is another powerful way to cultivate mindfulness. These practices combine movement and breath work to help you stay present and focused in the moment.

You don't have to be an expert to practice mindful movement. There are many beginner-friendly classes and videos

available online, or you can simply move your body in a way
that feels good to you while paying attention to your breath
and physical sensations.

Mindful Listening

Finally, mindful listening is a powerful way to cultivate
mindfulness in your relationships with others. To practice
mindful listening, simply give the other person your full attention and listen to them without judgment or distraction.
Pay attention to their words, tone of voice, and body language, and try to understand their perspective without in-
terrupting or interjecting with your own thoughts or opinions.

Practicing mindful listening can help you to improve your
relationships with others and develop greater empathy and
compassion.

Conclusion

Cultivating mindfulness is a powerful way to achieve enduring happiness and inner peace. By practicing mindfulness
regularly, you can reduce stress and anxiety, improve emo-

tional regulation and cognitive function, and enhance your overall well-being.

In this chapter, we've explored the science behind mindfulness and offered practical strategies for incorporating mindfulness into your daily life. Whether you choose to practice mindful breathing, mindful eating, mindful movement, or mindful listening, the key is to approach each moment with a sense of presence and non-judgment.

As you continue to cultivate mindfulness in your life, you'll find that you're better able to handle life's challenges with grace and ease, and that you're able to experience greater joy and contentment in each moment. So why not give mindfulness a try today and see for yourself the transformative power of being present?

08: The Art of Letting Go: Releasing the Past and Embracing the Present

Letting go of the past is one of the most challenging things anyone can do. Memories of past failures, losses, and traumatic experiences can linger in our minds, causing emotional pain and stress. These negative emotions can hold us back from achieving our goals, limit our potential, and prevent us from living a fulfilling life. However, the art of letting go can help us release these negative emotions and embrace the present moment. In this chapter, we will discuss how to let go of the past and achieve inner peace.

The first step in letting go of the past is to acknowledge and accept your emotions. It is natural to feel anger, sadness, and frustration when something bad happens to us. Instead of suppressing these emotions, it is essential to allow yourself to feel them. You can cry, scream, or talk to a trusted friend or therapist about your feelings. The key is to express your emotions in a healthy way and not let them consume you.

The second step is to identify the root cause of your negative emotions. It could be a specific event, person, or situation that triggered your emotions. Once you have identified the cause, it is essential to forgive yourself and others. Forgiveness is not about condoning someone's behavior or forgetting what happened. It is about letting go of the anger and resentment that you are holding onto and moving forward.

The third step is to reframe your thoughts. Negative thoughts and beliefs can keep you stuck in the past. Instead, focus on positive thoughts and beliefs that support your growth and well-being. For example, instead of dwelling on past failures, focus on what you learned from those experiences and how you can use that knowledge to achieve your goals.

The fourth step is to practice mindfulness. Mindfulness is the art of being present in the moment and observing your thoughts and emotions without judgment. It can help you stay grounded in the present and let go of negative thoughts and emotions from the past.

The fifth step is to create new positive experiences. Engage in activities that bring you joy and fulfillment, such as spending time with loved ones, pursuing a hobby, or volunteering. These positive experiences can help shift your focus from the past to the present and create new memories to cherish.

The sixth step is to practice gratitude. Gratitude is the practice of being thankful for what you have in your life. It can help shift your focus from what you have lost in the past to what you have in the present. You can practice gratitude by keeping a gratitude journal, expressing gratitude to others, or simply taking a moment to appreciate the beauty around you.

The seventh step is to seek professional help if needed. Letting go of the past can be challenging, and it is okay to seek help from a therapist or counselor. They can provide you with tools and strategies to help you cope with negative emotions and let go of the past.

The art of letting go is not an easy process, and it takes time and practice. However, the rewards of letting go of the past are endless. It can help you achieve inner peace, reduce stress, and improve your overall well-being. By following these steps, you can begin the journey of letting go of the past and embracing the present moment. Remember, life is

08: THE ART OF LETTING GO: RELEASING THE PAST AND EMBRACING THE PRESENT

too short to dwell on the past. Embrace the present and live your life to the fullest.

09: The Joy of Connection: Building and Nurturing Relationships

Humans are social beings. We are wired to connect with others and form relationships. From the moment we are born, we seek out human connection, and it remains an essential part of our lives until the end. Research shows that social connection is vital to our physical and mental well-being. People who have strong, supportive relationships are happier, healthier, and live longer than those who do not.

But building and nurturing relationships is not always easy. Many people struggle to form deep connections with others, while others find it challenging to maintain them. Fortunately, there are science-backed strategies and mindset shifts that can help you build and nurture relationships that bring joy and fulfillment to your life.

In this chapter, we will explore the joy of connection and the ways in which you can build and nurture meaningful relationships.

The Importance of Connection

Connection is a fundamental human need. We are social

creatures, and without social interaction, we can suffer from loneliness and isolation. Research shows that people who feel socially isolated or lonely are more likely to suffer from depression, anxiety, and other mental health issues. They are also at a higher risk of developing physical health problems such as heart disease, high blood pressure, and obesity.

On the other hand, people who have strong social connections are happier and healthier. They have better self-esteem, are more resilient in the face of stress, and live longer. Strong social connections also provide a sense of belonging and purpose, which can help us navigate life's challenges with greater ease.

Building Relationships

Building relationships is a process that requires time, effort, and patience. It is not something that happens overnight, and it requires ongoing attention and care. Here are some science-backed strategies for building relationships:

Be Authentic: Authenticity is key to building relationships. Be yourself, and don't try to be someone you're not. People are more likely to connect with you when you are genuine and authentic.

Listen: Listening is an essential part of building relationships. When you listen to others, you show that you value and respect them. You also gain valuable insights into their perspectives and experiences, which can help you build stronger connections.

Share: Sharing your own experiences, thoughts, and feelings can help build trust and rapport. It can also help you find common ground with others and strengthen your connections.

Be Vulnerable: Vulnerability is a crucial element of building deep connections. When you open up and share your fears, insecurities, and struggles, you show that you trust the other person and are willing to be vulnerable. This can help build trust and intimacy in the relationship.

Be Positive: Positivity is contagious. When you approach relationships with a positive attitude, you attract positive people and experiences into your life. Focus on the good in others, and celebrate their successes and accomplishments.

09: THE JOY OF CONNECTION: BUILDING AND NURTURING RELATIONSHIPS

Nurturing Relationships

Once you have formed a relationship, it is essential to nurture and maintain it. Relationships require ongoing care and attention to thrive. Here are some science-backed strategies for nurturing relationships:

Stay Connected: Regular communication is key to maintaining relationships. Whether it's through phone calls, text messages, or face-to-face interactions, make sure to stay in touch with the people you care about.

Show Appreciation: Expressing gratitude and appreciation can help strengthen relationships. Take the time to acknowledge the people in your life and the things they do for you. Let them know that you value and appreciate them.

Be Supportive: Supporting others through their challenges and struggles can help deepen your connections. Whether it's offering a listening ear, providing practical assistance, or offering words of encouragement, showing up for others is an essential part of nurturing relationships.

Practice Forgiveness: Conflict is a natural part of any relationship. Learning to forgive and let go of grudges can help heal wounds and strengthen relationships. Holding onto anger and resentment can damage relationships and cause long-term harm. Learning to forgive and move forward can help you maintain healthy relationships with others.

Respect Boundaries: Respecting others' boundaries is an important part of nurturing relationships. Everyone has different comfort levels and expectations when it comes to relationships. Be mindful of others' boundaries, and communicate your own boundaries clearly to avoid misunderstandings or hurt feelings.

Invest Time: Nurturing relationships takes time and effort. Set aside time in your schedule to spend with the people you care about. Whether it's a regular date night with your partner or a weekly phone call with a friend, investing time in your relationships can help strengthen them over time.

Mindset Shifts

In addition to these science-backed strategies, there are also mindset shifts that can help you build and nurture meaningful relationships.

09: THE JOY OF CONNECTION: BUILDING AND NURTURING RELATIONSHIPS

Focus on Quality, Not Quantity: When it comes to relationships, it's not about the number of friends you have, but the quality of those relationships. Focus on building deep, meaningful connections with a few people rather than superficial connections with many.

Let Go of Perfectionism: No one is perfect, and neither are relationships. Let go of the idea that relationships should be perfect or easy all the time. Embrace the ups and downs of relationships as a natural part of the process.

Embrace Vulnerability: Vulnerability can be scary, but it's also a powerful tool for building relationships. Embrace vulnerability as a way to connect with others on a deeper level and build trust.

Practice Gratitude: Gratitude can help you maintain a positive attitude and strengthen your relationships. Take the time to express gratitude for the people in your life and the things they do for you.

Be Open to Change: Relationships are dynamic and constantly evolving. Be open to change and growth in your relationships, and embrace new experiences and opportunities for connection.

Conclusion

Building and nurturing meaningful relationships is essential to our happiness and well-being. By practicing science-
backed strategies and mindset shifts, we can create connections that bring joy and fulfillment to our lives. Remember,
relationships require time, effort, and patience, but the rewards are well worth it. Embrace the joy of connection and
start building meaningful relationships today.

10: The Beauty of Diversity: Embracing Differences and Celebrating Uniqueness

The world is a beautiful, diverse place. Everywhere we look, we see different people, cultures, and ways of life. But despite this diversity, we often find ourselves struggling to accept and celebrate these differences. Instead, we tend to focus on what divides us, rather than what unites us. This lack of acceptance can lead to negative feelings such as prejudice, discrimination, and even hate.

In this chapter, we will explore the beauty of diversity and how embracing differences can lead to a more joyful and fulfilling life. We'll look at the science behind why we tend to resist diversity, and we'll offer some practical strategies for shifting our mindset and embracing the uniqueness of others.

Understanding Why We Resist Diversity

Despite our best intentions, we often find ourselves resisting diversity. Why is this? One reason is that we tend to view the world through the lens of our own experiences and beliefs. We are naturally drawn to people who share similar backgrounds, interests, and values as ourselves. This creates a sense of familiarity and comfort, which can be difficult to let go of.

Another reason we resist diversity is that we tend to categorize people into groups. We create stereotypes based on superficial characteristics such as race, gender, and religion. These stereotypes can be harmful because they limit our understanding of individuals and can lead to discrimination.

Finally, we often fear what we do not understand. When we encounter people who are different from us, we may feel uneasy or unsure of how to interact with them. This fear can lead to avoidance or hostility, which can further perpetuate prejudice and discrimination.

The Benefits of Embracing Diversity

Despite these challenges, embracing diversity can lead to a wealth of benefits. For one, it allows us to broaden our understanding of the world. When we interact with people who have different experiences and perspectives, we gain new insights and learn about different ways of living. This can be enriching and enlightening, expanding our understanding of what it means to be human.

Embracing diversity can also foster empathy and compassion. When we take the time to get to know people who are different from us, we begin to see their struggles and challenges. This can help us to appreciate the common humanity that binds us all together. It can also inspire us to take action to support and uplift others.

Finally, embracing diversity can lead to greater creativity and innovation. When we bring together people with different perspectives and experiences, we open up new possibilities for problem-solving and innovation. This can lead to breakthroughs in science, art, and technology that benefit all of humanity.

Strategies for Embracing Diversity

If you're ready to embrace diversity and celebrate the uniqueness of others, here are some strategies to get you started:

Challenge Your Stereotypes: Take some time to reflect on your own biases and stereotypes. Ask yourself where these beliefs come from and whether they are based on accurate information. Challenge yourself to see individuals as individuals, rather than representatives of a particular group.

Seek Out Diversity: Make an effort to seek out diverse experiences and perspectives. Attend events that celebrate different cultures, read books by authors from different backgrounds, and seek out opportunities to connect with people who are different from you.

Listen and Learn: When you encounter someone who is different from you, take the time to listen and learn. Ask questions and show a genuine interest in their experiences and perspectives. This can help to break down barriers and build connections.

Practice Empathy: Put yourself in the shoes of others and try to understand their experiences and challenges. This can help you to develop empathy and compassion for others.

Appreciate Differences: Rather than focusing on what divides us, focus on the things that make us unique. Appreciate the differences that make each person special and celebrate the diversity that makes our world so vibrant.

10: THE BEAUTY OF DIVERSITY: EMBRACING DIFFERENCES AND CELEBRATING UNIQUENESS

Speak Out Against Prejudice: When you encounter prejudice or discrimination, speak out against it. Use your voice to stand up for those who are marginalized or oppressed.

Practice Inclusivity: Make an effort to include people from different backgrounds and experiences in your life. Invite them into your social circles, listen to their stories, and make them feel welcome.

Educate Yourself: Educate yourself on issues of diversity and inclusion. Read books and articles, attend workshops and seminars, and engage in discussions about diversity and inclusion.

Take Action: Finally, take action to promote diversity and inclusion in your community. Volunteer for organizations that support marginalized groups, donate to causes that promote equity and justice, and advocate for policies that promote diversity and inclusion.

Conclusion

Embracing diversity is not always easy, but it is essential for creating a more joyful and fulfilling life. By challenging our

biases, seeking out diverse experiences, and practicing empathy and inclusivity, we can begin to appreciate the beauty
of our differences and celebrate the unique gifts that each
person brings to the world. With a little effort and a willingness to learn and grow, we can create a more inclusive and
compassionate world where all people are valued and re-
spected.

11: The Power of Positive Thinking: Transforming Your Mindset for Success

The human mind is a complex and powerful tool that can either make or break us. Our thoughts, beliefs, and attitudes shape our reality and influence our actions. If we can learn to harness the power of our minds, we can achieve incredible things and experience enduring happiness.

Positive thinking is a mindset shift that has the potential to transform our lives. It's about focusing on the good things in life and cultivating a positive outlook, even in the face of challenges and difficulties. Positive thinking is not about denying or ignoring the negative aspects of life but rather about choosing to see the good and focusing on solutions instead of problems.

In this chapter, we will explore the power of positive thinking and how it can help you achieve success and happiness in all areas of your life. We'll cover the science behind positive thinking, the benefits it offers, and practical strategies to cultivate a positive mindset.

The Science Behind Positive Thinking

11: THE POWER OF POSITIVE THINKING: TRANSFORMING YOUR MINDSET FOR SUCCESS

Positive thinking is not just a feel-good concept; it has a scientific basis. Research has shown that our thoughts and emotions have a profound impact on our physical and mental health, as well as our relationships and overall well-being.

Studies have found that people who have a positive outlook on life are more resilient, have better coping skills, and are less likely to experience depression and anxiety. They also have better cardiovascular health, a stronger immune system, and live longer.

One of the most significant findings in the field of positive psychology is the concept of neuroplasticity. Neuroplasticity refers to the brain's ability to reorganize itself in response to new experiences and learning. This means that we can literally rewire our brains by changing our thoughts and beliefs.

When we engage in positive thinking, we activate the brain's reward center and release feel-good neurotransmitters like dopamine and serotonin. These chemicals not only make us feel good but also improve our cognitive function, memory, and decision-making abilities.

11: THE POWER OF POSITIVE THINKING: TRANSFORM-ING YOUR MINDSET FOR SUCCESS

On the other hand, negative thinking triggers the stress response, which releases cortisol and other stress hormones that can damage our health over time. Chronic stress has been linked to a host of health problems, including heart disease, diabetes, and obesity.

The Benefits of Positive Thinking

Positive thinking offers a wealth of benefits that can help you achieve success and happiness in all areas of your life. Here are some of the ways that a positive mindset can benefit you:

Improved Mental Health: Positive thinking can help reduce symptoms of depression and anxiety and improve overall mental well-being.

Better Relationships: A positive mindset can improve communication, enhance empathy, and foster stronger relationships.

Increased Resilience: Positive thinking can help you bounce back from setbacks and challenges and stay motivated in the face of adversity.

11: THE POWER OF POSITIVE THINKING: TRANSFORM-ING YOUR MINDSET FOR SUCCESS

Improved Physical Health: Positive thinking has been linked to better cardiovascular health, a stronger immune system, and improved longevity.

Enhanced Creativity and Productivity: Positive thinking can boost your creativity and productivity by enhancing your problem-solving skills and decision-making abilities.

Practical Strategies for Cultivating Positive Thinking

Now that we've covered the science and benefits of positive thinking let's explore some practical strategies for cultivating a positive mindset:

Practice Gratitude: Gratitude is the practice of focusing on the good things in life and being thankful for them. Start each day by reflecting on three things you're grateful for, and take time to appreciate the people and experiences that bring you joy.

Reframe Negative Thoughts: When negative thoughts arise, reframe them in a positive light. For example, instead of saying, "I'm not good enough," say, "I'm learning and growing every day."

11: THE POWER OF POSITIVE THINKING: TRANSFORMING YOUR MINDSET FOR SUCCESS

Surround Yourself with Positivity: Spend time with people who uplift and inspire you, and avoid those who bring you down. Listen to positive music, read uplifting books, and watch inspiring movies and TV shows.

Practice Mindfulness: Mindfulness is the practice of being present and fully engaged in the current moment. It can help reduce stress and anxiety and cultivate a sense of calm and inner peace. Try practicing mindfulness meditation or simply focus on your breath and sensations throughout the day.

Set Realistic Goals: Set realistic goals that are achievable and align with your values and interests. Celebrate your progress along the way and stay focused on your purpose and vision.

Practice Self-Compassion: Treat yourself with kindness and compassion, just as you would treat a dear friend. Be gentle with yourself and practice self-care regularly, whether it's taking a hot bath, going for a walk in nature, or indulging in your favorite hobby.

Visualize Success: Use the power of visualization to imagine yourself succeeding and achieving your goals. Visualize yourself overcoming obstacles and facing challenges with confidence and grace.

Focus on Solutions: When faced with a problem or challenge, focus on finding solutions instead of dwelling on the problem itself. Brainstorm potential solutions and take action towards implementing them.

Practice Positive Self-Talk: Use positive affirmations and self-talk to boost your confidence and self-esteem. Repeat positive phrases like "I am capable and deserving of success" or "I am worthy and loved" to yourself daily.

Practice Random Acts of Kindness: Performing random acts of kindness can boost your mood and increase your sense of connection and community. It can be as simple as buying a coffee for a stranger or volunteering at a local charity.

In conclusion, the power of positive thinking is real, and it can have a profound impact on our lives. By cultivating a positive mindset, we can improve our mental and physical health, enhance our relationships, and achieve greater success and happiness in all areas of our lives. Use these science-backed strategies to unleash your inner joy and achieve lasting euphoria.

12: The Role of Self-Compassion in Achieving Enduring Happiness

Introduction:

Happiness is a state of mind that everyone desires to achieve. However, it's not a constant state and can fluctuate depending on life circumstances. Moreover, the pressure to always be happy and the constant comparison to others can lead to feelings of inadequacy and self-doubt. In such situations, self-compassion can play a crucial role in maintaining enduring happiness. In this chapter, we will explore the concept of self-compassion and its benefits in achieving lasting joy.

Understanding Self-Compassion:

Self-compassion can be defined as treating ourselves with the same kindness and care that we would offer to a friend going through a difficult time. It's about acknowledging our struggles and challenges without judgment and responding with kindness, support, and understanding.

According to Dr. Kristin Neff, a leading researcher on self-compassion, it consists of three elements:

12: THE ROLE OF SELF-COMPASSION IN ACHIEVING ENDURING HAPPINESS

Self-kindness: Being gentle and understanding with ourselves instead of being critical and judgmental.

Common humanity: Recognizing that we are not alone in our struggles and that others go through similar challenges.

Mindfulness: Being aware of our thoughts and emotions without getting caught up in them.

Benefits of Self-Compassion:

Practicing self-compassion has numerous benefits for our mental and physical well-being. Here are some of them:

Reduces stress: Self-compassion can help us manage stress better by reducing the negative impact of stress hormones on our body.

Boosts resilience: It helps us bounce back from setbacks and challenges with greater ease and adaptability.

Improves self-esteem: By being kind to ourselves, we develop a positive self-image and a greater sense of self-worth.

Enhances relationships: Self-compassion can improve our

relationships by reducing self-criticism and increasing empathy and understanding towards others.

Increases happiness: By cultivating a kinder and more compassionate attitude towards ourselves, we can experience greater joy and satisfaction in life.

Developing Self-Compassion:

Self-compassion is a skill that can be developed through practice and conscious effort. Here are some strategies to help you cultivate self-compassion:

Self-compassionate self-talk: Instead of criticizing ourselves for our mistakes, we can talk to ourselves with kindness and understanding. For instance, instead of saying, "I'm such an idiot for making this mistake," we can say, "It's okay to make mistakes. I'm doing my best."

Mindful self-awareness: We can develop self-compassion by becoming more aware of our thoughts and emotions without judgment. Mindfulness practices such as meditation and deep breathing can help us become more present and compassionate towards ourselves.

12: THE ROLE OF SELF-COMPASSION IN ACHIEVING ENDURING HAPPINESS

Practicing self-care: Taking care of ourselves physically, emotionally, and mentally is a powerful way to show ourselves kindness and compassion. This can include eating healthy, getting enough sleep, and engaging in activities that bring us joy and relaxation.

Cultivating gratitude: Focusing on the positive aspects of our life can help us develop a more compassionate and grateful attitude towards ourselves. We can start by listing the things we are grateful for each day and savoring the good moments.

Conclusion:

Self-compassion is a powerful tool for achieving enduring happiness. By treating ourselves with kindness and understanding, we can reduce stress, boost resilience, improve self-esteem, enhance relationships, and increase happiness. Developing self-compassion requires practice and effort, but the benefits are well worth it. So, let's start cultivating self-compassion and unleash our inner joy.

13: The Mind-Body Connection: The Impact of Physical Health on Mental Well-Being

In today's fast-paced world, mental health has become a critical issue, with depression and anxiety affecting millions of people globally. While many people are aware of the importance of mental health, few realize the significant impact that physical health has on mental well-being. In this chapter, we will explore the mind-body connection and how physical health affects mental well-being.

The mind-body connection is a complex relationship between the mind and body, where physical health can influence mental well-being and vice versa. The connection has been recognized for thousands of years, with ancient civilizations using various physical practices to improve mental well-being. Today, we have a better understanding of the connection, with scientific studies providing evidence of the impact of physical health on mental well-being.

Physical exercise is one of the most significant ways to improve mental well-being. Studies have shown that physical exercise releases endorphins, which are chemicals in the brain that improve mood and reduce stress levels. Physical exercise can also improve sleep quality, which has a significant impact on mental well-being. A lack of sleep can lead to fatigue, irritability, and mood swings, which can contribute to depression and anxiety.

Physical exercise also has long-term benefits for mental health. Studies have shown that regular exercise can reduce the risk of depression and anxiety in the long term. It can also improve cognitive function, memory, and concentration, which are essential for mental well-being.

In addition to physical exercise, nutrition is another crucial factor in the mind-body connection. A balanced diet that includes plenty of fruits, vegetables, and whole grains can provide the nutrients necessary for good mental health. Studies have shown that certain vitamins and minerals, such as vitamin D and omega-3 fatty acids, can improve mental well-being.

On the other hand, an unhealthy diet can have a negative impact on mental health. Diets that are high in processed foods, sugar, and saturated fats have been linked to depression and anxiety. It is essential to maintain a balanced and healthy diet to improve mental well-being.

Sleep is another critical factor in the mind-body connection. A lack of sleep can lead to physical and mental health problems, including depression, anxiety, and weight gain. Sleep is essential for the body to repair and regenerate, and a lack of sleep can lead to chronic fatigue, which can contribute to depression and anxiety.

Stress is another factor that affects the mind-body connection. Stress can have a significant impact on physical and mental health, leading to various health problems such as heart disease, diabetes, and depression. It is essential to manage stress through various techniques, such as mindfulness meditation, deep breathing, and yoga.

Social connections are also an essential factor in the mind-body connection. Studies have shown that social connections can improve mental well-being and reduce the risk of depression and anxiety. It is important to maintain social connections, whether through family, friends, or community groups, to improve mental well-being.

In addition to physical health, mental health can also have

an impact on physical health. Depression and anxiety have been linked to various physical health problems, including heart disease, diabetes, and obesity. It is essential to maintain good mental health to improve physical health.

In conclusion, the mind-body connection is a complex relationship between physical health and mental well-being. Physical exercise, nutrition, sleep, stress management, and social connections are all essential factors in the mind-body connection. It is important to maintain a healthy lifestyle to improve mental well-being and reduce the risk of depression and anxiety.

14: The Importance of Sleep: The Role of Rest and Recovery in Achieving Euphoria

Introduction

In our fast-paced and hyper-connected world, getting enough sleep seems like a luxury. Many of us prioritize work, family, and social obligations over sleep, thinking that sacrificing a few hours of shut-eye won't harm our productivity or overall well-being. However, the truth is, getting enough quality sleep is crucial to achieving lasting happiness and euphoria. In this chapter, we'll delve into the science of sleep and explore its vital role in our physical, mental, and emotional health.

The Basics of Sleep

Before we discuss the importance of sleep, let's first understand what it is and how it works. Sleep is a natural and essential state of rest in which our body and mind undergo critical processes of repair, restoration, and consolidation of memories and learning. When we sleep, our brain enters a series of distinct stages, each with its unique characteristics and functions.

14: THE IMPORTANCE OF SLEEP: THE ROLE OF REST AND RECOVERY IN ACHIEVING EUPHORIA

The first stage is a light sleep phase where our body gradually relaxes, and our brain activity starts to slow down. The second stage is a deeper sleep phase where our brainwaves become slower, and our body temperature and heart rate decrease. In the third and fourth stages, we enter a deep sleep phase, also known as slow-wave sleep, characterized by the slowest brainwaves and the most profound physical and mental rest. Finally, we enter the rapid eye movement (REM) phase, where our brain activity increases, and we experience vivid dreams and memory consolidation.

The ideal sleep cycle consists of around 90 minutes of non-REM and REM phases, repeating itself four to six times per night. A typical adult needs between seven to nine hours of sleep per night to function optimally, although some individuals may require more or less sleep depending on their age, genetics, and lifestyle factors.

The Physical Benefits of Sleep

Getting enough sleep is crucial for our physical health, as it affects nearly every system in our body. During sleep, our body undergoes essential processes of repair, maintenance, and growth, including:

14: THE IMPORTANCE OF SLEEP: THE ROLE OF REST AND RECOVERY IN ACHIEVING EUPHORIA

– The release of growth hormones, which promote tissue repair and muscle development

– The regulation of appetite and metabolism, which affect our weight and risk of chronic diseases

– The restoration of the immune system, which defends against infections and diseases

– The maintenance of cardiovascular health, which lowers the risk of heart attacks, strokes, and hypertension

– The reduction of inflammation and oxidative stress, which prevent cellular damage and aging

On the other hand, sleep deprivation or poor sleep quality can lead to a range of physical health problems, such as:

– Obesity and metabolic disorders

– Cardiovascular diseases

– Diabetes

– Weakened immune system

– Increased risk of infections and illnesses

– Chronic pain and inflammation

The Mental and Emotional Benefits of Sleep

Sleep also plays a crucial role in our mental and emotional health, affecting our mood, cognitive function, and social behavior. During sleep, our brain consolidates memories and learning, strengthens neural connections, and filters out irrelevant information, preparing us for the next day's challenges.

Getting enough sleep is associated with:

– Better mood and emotional regulation

– Improved cognitive function, such as memory, attention, and problem-solving

– Enhanced creativity and insight

– Reduced stress and anxiety

– Better social interaction and communication

14: THE IMPORTANCE OF SLEEP: THE ROLE OF REST AND RECOVERY IN ACHIEVING EUPHORIA

In contrast, sleep deprivation or poor sleep quality can lead to:

– Mood disorders, such as depression and anxiety

– Cognitive impairment, such as forgetfulness, lack of concentration, and poor decision-making

– Reduced creativity and problem-solving abilities

– Increased stress and irritability

– Poor social skills and communication

Tips for Improving Sleep Quality

Now that we've established the vital role of sleep in achieving euphoria and overall well-being, let's explore some science-backed strategies for improving sleep quality and quantity:

Stick to a sleep schedule: Try to go to bed and wake up at the same time every day, even on weekends or holidays, to regulate your internal clock.

Create a sleep-conducive environment: Make sure your bedroom is cool, dark, quiet, and comfortable, with a supportive mattress and pillows.

Limit exposure to electronic devices: Avoid using electronic devices such as smartphones, tablets, or laptops before bedtime, as they emit blue light that suppresses melatonin production and disrupts sleep.

Avoid stimulants and sedatives: Limit your consumption of caffeine, nicotine, alcohol, and sedatives, as they can interfere with sleep quality and disrupt your natural sleep cycle.

Exercise regularly: Regular physical activity can improve sleep quality and reduce sleep onset latency, but avoid exercising too close to bedtime, as it may increase arousal and delay sleep onset.

Practice relaxation techniques: Try mindfulness meditation, progressive muscle relaxation, deep breathing, or yoga before bedtime to calm your mind and body and promote sleep.

Avoid napping: While napping can be beneficial for some individuals, it can disrupt your sleep cycle and make it harder to fall asleep at night, especially if you have insomnia.

Seek treatment for sleep disorders: If you have chronic sleep problems, such as sleep apnea, restless leg syndrome, or insomnia, consult a healthcare professional for diagnosis and treatment options.

Conclusion

Sleep is an essential and often underestimated aspect of our physical, mental, and emotional health. Getting enough quality sleep is crucial to achieving lasting happiness and euphoria, as it affects nearly every system in our body and mind. By following science-backed strategies for improving sleep quality and quantity, we can unleash our inner joy and achieve enduring happiness. So, make sleep a priority in your life and enjoy the benefits of rest and recovery.

15: The Science of Nutrition: How What You Eat Affects Your Mood

Nutrition plays a crucial role in our physical health, but did you know that it also has a significant impact on our mental well-being? What we eat can influence our mood, energy levels, and even our ability to cope with stress. In this chapter, we will explore the science behind the connection between nutrition and mood and learn how we can use this knowledge to unleash our inner joy and achieve enduring happiness.

To understand the relationship between nutrition and mood, we need to look at the role of neurotransmitters in our brain. Neurotransmitters are chemicals that transmit signals between neurons, or nerve cells, in the brain. There are several neurotransmitters involved in regulating our mood, including serotonin, dopamine, and norepinephrine.

Serotonin is often referred to as the "happy hormone" because it plays a key role in regulating mood, appetite, and sleep. Low levels of serotonin have been linked to depression and anxiety, while high levels are associated with feelings of well-being and happiness. Our body produces serotonin from the amino acid tryptophan, which we get from protein-rich foods such as chicken, turkey, fish, and eggs.

Dopamine is another neurotransmitter that is involved in regulating mood, motivation, and pleasure. Low levels of dopamine have been linked to depression, while high levels are associated with feelings of joy and excitement. Our body produces dopamine from the amino acid tyrosine, which we get from protein-rich foods such as meat, dairy, and soy products.

Norepinephrine is a neurotransmitter that is involved in the "fight or flight" response, which is the body's response to stress. Low levels of norepinephrine have been linked to depression, while high levels can cause anxiety and agitation. Our body produces norepinephrine from the amino acid phenylalanine, which we get from protein-rich foods such as meat, fish, eggs, and dairy products.

Now that we understand the role of neurotransmitters in regulating our mood, let's take a closer look at how different nutrients can affect our mental well-being.

Carbohydrates are the primary source of energy for our body and brain. Complex carbohydrates, such as whole grains, fruits, and vegetables, are broken down slowly, providing a steady supply of energy throughout the day. Simple carbohydrates, such as sugar and refined flour, are broken down quickly, causing a rapid spike in blood sugar levels followed by a crash. This can lead to mood swings, irritability, and fatigue.

Protein is essential for building and repairing tissues in our body, including the brain. As we mentioned earlier, protein is also a source of the amino acids tryptophan, tyrosine, and phenylalanine, which are precursors to neurotransmitters involved in regulating mood.

Omega-3 fatty acids are a type of healthy fat that is essential for brain function and development. Studies have shown that omega-3 fatty acids can help reduce symptoms of depression and anxiety. Good sources of omega-3 fatty acids include fatty fish such as salmon, tuna, and mackerel, as well as walnuts, flaxseeds, and chia seeds.

B vitamins, particularly folate and B12, are important for brain function and the production of neurotransmitters such as serotonin and dopamine. Low levels of these vitamins have been linked to depression and other mood disorders. Good sources of folate include leafy greens, legumes, and fortified cereals. Good sources of B12 include meat, fish, eggs, and dairy products.

Vitamin D is a vitamin that is essential for bone health and immune function. It is also involved in regulating mood. Low levels of vitamin D have been linked to depression, particularly in people who live in areas with limited sunlight. Good sources of vitamin D include fatty fish, fortified dairy products, and exposure to sunlight.

In addition to the specific nutrients mentioned above, it's important to maintain a balanced and varied diet to ensure that you're getting all the nutrients your body and brain need. A diet that is high in processed foods, sugar, and unhealthy fats can contribute to inflammation in the body, which has been linked to depression and other mood disorders.

In addition to choosing the right foods, it's also important to pay attention to how and when you eat. Skipping meals or going long periods without eating can cause your blood sugar levels to drop, which can lead to mood swings, irritability, and fatigue. Eating smaller, more frequent meals throughout the day can help maintain steady blood sugar levels and provide a steady supply of energy to your brain and body.

Another important factor to consider is hydration. Dehydration can cause headaches, fatigue, and irritability, which can all contribute to a negative mood. Make sure to drink plenty of water throughout the day to stay hydrated and keep your body and brain functioning at their best.

While nutrition is an important factor in promoting mental well-being, it's important to note that it's not a cure-all. If you're struggling with depression, anxiety, or other mood disorders, it's important to seek professional help. A mental health professional can provide you with the support and resources you need to manage your symptoms and improve your overall well-being.

In conclusion, the science of nutrition teaches us that what we eat can have a significant impact on our mood and mental well-being. By choosing nutrient-dense foods that support brain function and regulate neurotransmitters, we can unleash our inner joy and achieve enduring happiness. By paying attention to how and when we eat, staying hydrated, and seeking professional help when needed, we can take control of our mental health and live our best lives.

16: The Joy of Movement: Harnessing the Power of Exercise for Euphoria

When it comes to finding joy and happiness, many of us tend to focus on external factors such as our relationships, career, or financial status. However, one of the most effective ways to achieve lasting euphoria is by harnessing the power of exercise. The benefits of regular physical activity go far beyond just physical health and can have a profound impact on our emotional and mental well-being.

In this chapter, we'll explore the science-backed benefits of exercise for euphoria and provide practical strategies for incorporating movement into your daily routine.

The Science of Exercise and Euphoria

Have you ever noticed how great you feel after a workout? Whether it's a long run or a yoga class, the endorphins released during physical activity can produce a euphoric state commonly known as "runner's high." But the benefits of exercise go far beyond just a temporary mood boost.

Research has shown that regular exercise can have a profound impact on our mental health, improving symptoms of depression, anxiety, and stress. This is due in part to the release of endorphins, which act as natural painkillers and mood elevators.

Additionally, exercise has been found to increase the production of brain-derived neurotrophic factor (BDNF), a protein that plays a critical role in the growth and development of neurons. BDNF has been linked to improved cognitive function, as well as a reduced risk of neurodegenerative diseases such as Alzheimer's.

Other benefits of exercise for euphoria include improved sleep, increased energy levels, and a greater sense of self-confidence and self-esteem. And while the physical benefits of exercise are often touted, the mental health benefits are just as important and can have a lasting impact on our overall well-being.

Strategies for Incorporating Movement into Your Daily Routine

Now that we've explored the science behind exercise and euphoria, let's dive into some practical strategies for incorporating movement into your daily routine.

Find an Activity You Enjoy

The key to sticking with any exercise routine is finding an activity that you enjoy. Whether it's running, yoga, or dancing, find a form of movement that feels good to you and that you look forward to doing.

Set Realistic Goals

When starting a new exercise routine, it's important to set realistic goals for yourself. This could be as simple as committing to a 30-minute walk each day or as ambitious as training for a marathon. By setting achievable goals, you'll build confidence in your ability to stick with your routine and achieve success.

Make Movement a Priority

We all lead busy lives, but it's important to prioritize movement in your daily routine. Whether it's waking up early to go for a run or taking a lunchtime yoga class, make movement a non-negotiable part of your day.

16: THE JOY OF MOVEMENT: HARNESSING THE POWER OF EXERCISE FOR EUPHORIA

Mix It Up

Variety is the spice of life, and it's also important for keeping your exercise routine interesting and challenging. Mix up your routine with a variety of activities such as cardio, strength training, and flexibility work.

Find a Support System

Having a support system can make all the difference when it comes to sticking with an exercise routine. Whether it's a workout buddy or an online community, find people who share your goals and can offer support and encouragement along the way.

Final Thoughts

The benefits of exercise for euphoria are clear, both in terms of physical and mental health. By incorporating movement into your daily routine and finding an activity that you enjoy, you can harness the power of exercise to achieve lasting happiness and well-being.

Remember to set realistic goals, prioritize movement in your day, mix up your routine, and find a support system to keep you motivated and on track. With a little dedication and a willingness to try new things, you can unleash your inner joy and achieve enduring happiness.

It's important to note that starting a new exercise routine can be daunting, especially if you're not used to being active. But remember that every journey begins with a single step, and even small changes can have a big impact on your overall health and happiness.

If you're struggling to find the motivation to get started, try setting yourself a challenge or signing up for a class or event that will keep you accountable. And remember that progress is not always linear - there will be setbacks and challenges along the way, but each one presents an opportunity to learn and grow.

Incorporating movement into your daily routine is just one of the many strategies for achieving euphoria and lasting happiness. But it's an important one, as the physical and mental health benefits of exercise can have a profound impact on your overall well-being.

So next time you're feeling stressed or overwhelmed, lace up your shoes or roll out your yoga mat and give yourself the gift of movement. Your body and mind will thank you for it.

17: The Benefits of Meditation: Finding Peace and Clarity of Mind

Meditation has been practiced for thousands of years and is often associated with Eastern spirituality and mysticism. However, in recent years, meditation has become increasingly popular in the Western world due to its numerous physical and mental health benefits.

Meditation is a practice that involves training your mind to focus and redirect your thoughts. It can be done in a variety of ways, such as sitting or lying down, closing your eyes, and focusing on your breath or a particular word or phrase. The goal of meditation is to increase awareness of the present moment, reduce stress, and promote relaxation.

One of the most significant benefits of meditation is its ability to reduce stress and anxiety. Meditation has been shown to decrease the levels of the stress hormone cortisol in the body, which can help alleviate symptoms of anxiety and depression. Studies have also found that meditation can improve sleep, reduce blood pressure, and boost the immune system.

Another benefit of meditation is its ability to enhance focus and concentration. Regular meditation practice can improve cognitive function, including memory, attention, and decision-making skills. This can be especially beneficial for those who have difficulty concentrating due to ADHD or other conditions.

Meditation can also improve emotional regulation and increase feelings of well-being. It can help individuals become more self-aware, develop greater empathy and compassion, and cultivate positive emotions such as gratitude and love.

In addition to these mental and emotional benefits, meditation can also have physical benefits. Studies have shown that regular meditation can lower the risk of heart disease, stroke, and other chronic conditions. It can also help reduce pain and inflammation in the body.

One of the most appealing aspects of meditation is that it can be done anywhere, at any time. It does not require any special equipment or training, and can be practiced by people of all ages and abilities. Even just a few minutes of meditation each day can have significant benefits for mental and physical health.

17: THE BENEFITS OF MEDITATION: FINDING PEACE AND CLARITY OF MIND

To get started with meditation, it is helpful to find a quiet, comfortable space where you will not be disturbed. Set a timer for the desired length of your meditation practice, and choose a focus for your attention, such as your breath or a mantra. Allow your mind to relax and simply observe your thoughts without judgment.

As you become more comfortable with meditation, you can experiment with different techniques, such as mindfulness meditation, loving-kindness meditation, or body scan meditation. You can also try meditating with a group or using guided meditations to help you stay focused.

In conclusion, meditation is a powerful tool for improving mental and physical health. By incorporating regular meditation practice into your daily routine, you can reduce stress and anxiety, improve focus and concentration, and increase feelings of well-being and happiness. Whether you are new to meditation or have been practicing for years, there is always more to learn and discover about this ancient practice. So why not give it a try and see how meditation can transform your life?

18: The Joy of Creativity: Tapping into Your Inner Artist

Introduction

Creativity is the soul's expression of freedom. It is a pathway to pure joy and a powerful tool to achieve euphoria. Creativity comes in many forms: painting, drawing, writing, singing, dancing, designing, and many more. It is not limited to artists, but it's a skill that can be honed and practiced by anyone who is willing to put in the effort.

In this chapter, we will explore the connection between creativity and euphoria, the science behind it, and practical tips to unleash your inner artist.

The Science Behind Creativity and Euphoria

When we engage in creative activities, our brain releases dopamine, a neurotransmitter associated with pleasure, motivation, and reward. Dopamine triggers the brain's pleasure center, producing a sense of euphoria, satisfaction, and happiness.

According to a study conducted by the National Endowment for the Arts, people who regularly engage in creative activities are more likely to report higher levels of happiness, better mental health, and overall well-being. Moreover, studies have shown that creative expression can be an effective tool to manage stress, anxiety, and depression.

The Benefits of Creativity

The benefits of creativity are numerous, and they go beyond the immediate pleasure and happiness that it provides. Creativity can help you:

Boost your self-esteem: Creating something that you're proud of can increase your self-confidence and sense of self-worth.

Reduce stress and anxiety: Engaging in creative activities can help you focus on the present moment, distract yourself from negative thoughts, and lower your cortisol levels.

Improve your mental health: Studies have shown that creative expression can be a powerful tool to manage symptoms of depression, anxiety, and PTSD.

Enhance your problem-solving skills: Creativity requires you to think outside the box and come up with innovative solutions, which can translate to improved problem-solving skills in your personal and professional life.

Strengthen your relationships: Participating in creative activities with others can help build deeper connections, increase empathy, and foster a sense of community.

Practical Tips to Unleash Your Inner Artist

Make time for creativity: Schedule regular time in your day or week to engage in creative activities. Whether it's a few minutes or a few hours, make it a priority.

Try something new: Challenge yourself to try something new and different. Experiment with different art forms or try a new technique in a familiar one.

Set realistic expectations: Don't put too much pressure on yourself to create a masterpiece. Instead, focus on the process and enjoy the journey.

Embrace mistakes: Creativity is not about perfection. Embrace mistakes as part of the learning process and allow yourself to experiment without fear of failure.

18: THE JOY OF CREATIVITY: TAPPING INTO YOUR INNER ARTIST

Find inspiration: Seek out inspiration from other artists, nature, or everyday life. Keep a sketchbook or inspiration board to collect ideas and references.

Join a community: Connect with other artists and creatives in your community or online. Join a local art group, attend workshops, or participate in online forums to get feedback, support, and inspiration.

Conclusion

Creativity is a powerful tool to achieve euphoria and enduring happiness. Whether you're an experienced artist or a beginner, incorporating creative activities into your life can improve your mental health, boost your self-esteem, and enhance your problem-solving skills.

By making time for creativity, trying something new, setting realistic expectations, embracing mistakes, finding inspiration, and joining a community, you can tap into your inner artist and unleash the joy of creativity.

19: Embracing Change: The Art of Adaptability and Growth

Change is a fundamental aspect of life, and it is something that we cannot escape. From our personal lives to the world at large, change is a constant factor, and how we choose to respond to it can significantly impact our level of happiness and overall well-being. The art of adaptability is essential in navigating life's changes, and it is a crucial component of achieving enduring happiness.

Embracing change can be challenging, especially when it is unexpected or unwanted. It is natural to feel anxious or scared when we are faced with something new or uncertain. However, it is essential to recognize that change can also bring about positive outcomes and opportunities for growth.

One of the keys to embracing change is having a growth mindset. This means believing that our abilities and skills can be developed through dedication and hard work. When we approach change with a growth mindset, we view challenges as opportunities to learn and improve ourselves.

In order to cultivate a growth mindset, it is essential to develop a sense of curiosity and openness to new experiences. Instead of resisting change, try to approach it with a sense of wonder and excitement. Ask questions and seek out new knowledge and perspectives. This can help you to view change as an opportunity to expand your horizons and learn something new.

Another important aspect of embracing change is being able to let go of the past. Holding onto old ways of thinking or behaving can limit your ability to adapt to new situations. It is essential to recognize that the past is gone, and the only thing we have control over is the present moment. When we let go of the past, we free ourselves up to embrace new experiences and opportunities.

Of course, change can also be challenging because it can be uncomfortable. It is natural to want to stay within our comfort zones, where things feel familiar and safe. However, this can also limit our ability to grow and experience new things. It is important to recognize that discomfort is a necessary part of growth and that it can lead to positive outcomes.

One way to embrace discomfort is to challenge yourself regularly. Set goals that are just beyond your current abilities, and work towards them consistently. This can help you to develop the resilience and confidence needed to navigate life's changes.

Another key to embracing change is developing a sense of resilience. Resilience refers to our ability to bounce back from setbacks or difficult experiences. When we develop resilience, we are better able to adapt to changes and overcome challenges.

There are many strategies for developing resilience, including building a strong support network, practicing self-care, and developing a sense of purpose or meaning in life. It is also essential to practice self-compassion and to be kind to yourself during difficult times.

Ultimately, the art of adaptability and growth is about approaching change with a positive attitude and an openness to new experiences. It is about recognizing that change can bring about both challenges and opportunities, and that it is up to us to choose how we respond. When we embrace change with a growth mindset and develop resilience, we can navigate life's changes with greater ease and achieve en-

19: EMBRACING CHANGE: THE ART OF ADAPTABILITY AND GROWTH

during happiness.

20: The Power of Forgiveness: Letting Go of Resentment and Finding Inner Peace

Forgiveness is a powerful act that can transform our lives, allowing us to let go of the pain and resentment that may be holding us back. It is often said that forgiveness is not for the person who hurt us, but for ourselves. By forgiving, we release ourselves from the burden of anger and resentment, and open ourselves up to joy, happiness, and peace.

However, forgiveness can be a difficult process, especially when we have been deeply hurt. We may feel that by forgiving, we are condoning the behavior of the person who hurt us, or that we are letting them off the hook. But forgiveness is not about forgetting or excusing the actions of others. It is about acknowledging the pain and hurt that we have experienced, and choosing to move forward in a way that empowers us.

The Benefits of Forgiveness

Forgiveness is not only a powerful tool for our emotional well-being, but it can also have positive effects on our physical health. Research has shown that forgiveness can lower blood pressure, reduce anxiety and depression, and improve overall immune function.

In addition, forgiveness can improve our relationships with others. When we forgive, we are able to let go of resentment and anger, which can often cause us to distance ourselves from those we care about. By choosing to forgive, we are able to open ourselves up to deeper connections with others, and to foster a sense of empathy and compassion that can lead to more positive interactions.

The Roadblocks to Forgiveness

Despite the many benefits of forgiveness, it can be a difficult process, especially when we have been deeply hurt. There are many roadblocks that can prevent us from forgiving, including:

Fear of being hurt again. When we have been hurt in the past, we may be afraid that if we forgive, we will be opening ourselves up to being hurt again.

A sense of injustice. When we have been wronged, we may feel that the other person does not deserve our forgiveness, and that by forgiving them, we are letting them off the hook.

Anger and resentment. When we are consumed by anger and resentment, it can be difficult to see the situation clearly and objectively, making forgiveness seem impossible.

A lack of empathy. When we are unable to see things from the other person's perspective, it can be difficult to understand why they acted the way they did, making forgiveness seem unlikely.

Overcoming Roadblocks to Forgiveness

While forgiveness can be a difficult process, there are many strategies that can help us overcome the roadblocks that may be preventing us from forgiving.

Practice empathy. Try to see the situation from the other person's perspective, and to understand why they may have acted the way they did. This can help us to let go of anger and resentment, and to see the situation more objectively.

Challenge negative thoughts. When we are consumed by negative thoughts and emotions, it can be difficult to see the situation clearly. Try to challenge these thoughts, and to re-frame the situation in a more positive light.

Set boundaries. While forgiveness is important, it is also important to set boundaries and to protect ourselves from further harm. This may involve limiting contact with the person who hurt us, or setting clear expectations for how we expect to be treated in the future.

Seek support. Forgiveness can be a difficult process, and it is important to seek support from friends, family, or a therapist who can help us to work through our feelings and emotions.

The Process of Forgiveness

The process of forgiveness is a deeply personal one, and it can look different for everyone. However, there are some common steps that can help us to move towards forgiveness and to find inner peace.

Acknowledge the hurt. The first step towards forgiveness is to acknowledge the pain and hurt that we have experienced. This can be a difficult step, as it requires us to confront the pain head-on. However, it is an important step in the process of healing and letting go of resentment.

Take responsibility for our own feelings. While the actions of others may have caused us pain, it is important to recognize that we are responsible for our own feelings and emotions. By taking ownership of our own feelings, we can begin to let go of the power that the other person may have had over us.

Practice empathy. As mentioned earlier, empathy is a key component of forgiveness. Try to see the situation from the other person's perspective, and to understand why they may have acted the way they did. This can help us to let go of anger and resentment, and to see the situation more objectively.

Choose to forgive. Forgiveness is a choice, and it is one that we must make for ourselves. This may involve letting go of the desire for revenge or retribution, and choosing to move forward with compassion and understanding.

Release the resentment. Once we have made the choice to forgive, it is important to release the resentment that we may be holding onto. This may involve practicing mindfulness, meditation, or other techniques to help us let go of negative emotions.

Set boundaries. While forgiveness is important, it is also important to set boundaries and to protect ourselves from further harm. This may involve limiting contact with the person who hurt us, or setting clear expectations for how we expect to be treated in the future.

Practice self-compassion. Forgiveness is a difficult process, and it is important to be kind and compassionate towards ourselves as we work through our emotions. This may involve self-care practices such as exercise, meditation, or spending time in nature.

Conclusion

Forgiveness is a powerful tool that can transform our lives, allowing us to let go of the pain and resentment that may be holding us back. While it can be a difficult process, there are many strategies that can help us to overcome the roadblocks that may be preventing us from forgiving. By choosing to forgive, we open ourselves up to joy, happiness, and peace, and create space for deeper connections with others. Re-member, forgiveness is not about forgetting or excusing the actions of others, but about acknowledging the pain and hurt that we have experienced, and choosing to move forward in a way that empowers us.

21: The Art of Self-Care: Prioritizing Your Needs and Nurturing Your Soul

As the saying goes, you can't pour from an empty cup. This is why self-care is crucial in achieving euphoria and enduring happiness. However, self-care goes beyond bubble baths and face masks. It encompasses a range of activities and practices that promote physical, mental, and emotional well-being.

In this chapter, we will dive deep into the art of self-care and explore science-backed strategies and mindset shifts that can help you prioritize your needs and nurture your soul.

Defining Self-Care

Self-care is the act of intentionally taking care of oneself. It is a proactive approach to wellness that involves engaging in activities that promote physical, mental, and emotional well-being. Self-care is not a selfish act, but rather a necessary one. It allows individuals to take charge of their health and happiness, reducing stress and burnout.

21: THE ART OF SELF-CARE: PRIORITIZING YOUR NEEDS AND NURTURING YOUR SOUL

The Importance of Self-Care

Self-care is essential for maintaining good health and well-being. Studies have shown that engaging in self-care activities can help reduce stress and improve mood, leading to better physical and mental health outcomes. Self-care can also boost confidence and self-esteem, promoting a positive self-image.

Moreover, practicing self-care can help prevent burnout, a state of emotional, physical, and mental exhaustion caused by chronic stress. Burnout can lead to a range of negative health outcomes, including depression, anxiety, and physical illness. Self-care can help individuals manage stress and prevent burnout, allowing them to perform at their best and enjoy life to the fullest.

Self-Care Strategies

There are many self-care strategies that individuals can use to promote physical, mental, and emotional well-being. Some of these include:

a. Physical Self-Care

21: THE ART OF SELF-CARE: PRIORITIZING YOUR NEEDS AND NURTURING YOUR SOUL

Physical self-care involves taking care of one's body. This can include engaging in regular exercise, getting enough sleep, and eating a healthy diet. It can also involve practicing good hygiene, such as showering regularly, brushing one's teeth, and washing one's hands.

b. Emotional Self-Care

Emotional self-care involves taking care of one's emotional well-being. This can include practicing mindfulness meditation, engaging in activities that bring joy, and seeking support from friends and family.

c. Mental Self-Care

Mental self-care involves taking care of one's mental health. This can include engaging in activities that promote cognitive health, such as reading, writing, and doing puzzles. It can also involve seeking support from mental health professionals, such as therapists or counselors.

d. Social Self-Care

Social self-care involves taking care of one's social well-being. This can include spending time with friends and family, engaging in social activities, and joining social clubs or groups.

e. Spiritual Self-Care

Spiritual self-care involves taking care of one's spiritual well-being. This can include engaging in religious or spiritual practices, such as attending church or meditating.

Mindset Shifts for Self-Care

In addition to engaging in self-care activities, individuals can also benefit from adopting certain mindset shifts. These include:

a. Prioritizing Self-Care

One of the most important mindset shifts for self-care is prioritizing it. This involves recognizing that self-care is essential for well-being and making it a non-negotiable part of one's routine.

b. Letting Go of Guilt

Many individuals struggle with guilt when engaging in self-care activities. However, it is essential to let go of this guilt and recognize that self-care is not selfish, but rather a necessary part of wellness.

c. Embracing Imperfection

Perfectionism can be a barrier to self-care. It can lead individuals to set unrealistic expectations for themselves, causing them to neglect their needs. Embracing imperfection and recognizing that self-care is a process, not a destination.

d. Practicing Self-Compassion

Self-compassion is the act of treating oneself with kindness and understanding, especially in times of difficulty. It involves recognizing that everyone makes mistakes and that it is okay to be imperfect. Practicing self-compassion can help individuals reduce self-judgment and promote self-care.

e. Setting Boundaries

Setting boundaries is essential for practicing self-care. It involves recognizing one's limits and communicating them to others. By setting boundaries, individuals can prevent burnout and ensure that they have time and energy for self-care.

Incorporating Self-Care into Your Routine

Incorporating self-care into one's routine can be challenging, especially for individuals with busy schedules. However, it is essential to make self-care a priority. Here are some tips for incorporating self-care into your routine:

a. Schedule Self-Care Activities

Scheduling self-care activities can help individuals make them a non-negotiable part of their routine. This can involve setting aside time each day or each week for self-care activities.

b. Start Small

Starting small can help individuals build momentum and develop the habit of self-care. This can involve engaging in small self-care activities, such as taking a 10-minute walk or meditating for 5 minutes.

c. Be Creative

21: THE ART OF SELF-CARE: PRIORITIZING YOUR NEEDS AND NURTURING YOUR SOUL

Self-care does not have to be expensive or time-consuming. There are many creative ways to engage in self-care, such as journaling, listening to music, or taking a relaxing bath.

d. Find What Works for You

Self-care is not a one-size-fits-all approach. It is essential to find self-care activities that work for you and bring you joy. This may involve trying out different activities and seeing what resonates with you.

e. Hold Yourself Accountable

Holding oneself accountable is essential for incorporating self-care into one's routine. This can involve tracking self-care activities, setting goals, and seeking support from friends and family.

Conclusion

Self-care is an essential aspect of achieving euphoria and enduring happiness. It involves taking care of oneself physically, mentally, emotionally, socially, and spiritually. By prioritizing self-care and adopting mindset shifts, individuals can reduce stress, prevent burnout, and promote well-being. Incorporating self-care into one's routine may take time and effort, but it is well worth it in the end. Remember, self-care is not selfish, but rather a necessary part of wellness.

22: The Joy of Giving: The Rewards of Generosity and Compassion

The joy of giving is one of the most powerful and rewarding experiences that human beings can have. It is a deeply meaningful and fulfilling act that not only benefits the recipient of our generosity but also brings us lasting happiness and inner peace. This chapter will explore the science behind giving and the many benefits that come from practicing generosity and compassion in our daily lives.

Generosity and compassion are two of the most essential qualities that define us as human beings. They are the foundation of our social interactions and the glue that holds our communities together. Research has shown that practicing these virtues can have a profound impact on our physical, emotional, and mental well-being.

When we give to others, whether it is our time, money, or resources, we activate the pleasure centers in our brain, releasing dopamine, serotonin, and oxytocin, the chemicals responsible for feelings of happiness, contentment, and connection. This flood of feel-good hormones not only makes us feel good in the moment but also creates a lasting sense of well-being and fulfillment.

Moreover, giving has been found to have a positive impact on our physical health. Studies have shown that people who engage in acts of kindness and generosity have lower levels of stress, inflammation, and blood pressure, leading to a reduced risk of chronic diseases such as heart disease, diabetes, and cancer.

One of the most significant benefits of giving is the sense of purpose and meaning it provides. When we give to others, we are contributing to something larger than ourselves, and this sense of connection to something bigger is essential for our overall well-being. It helps us feel like we are part of something meaningful and provides a sense of belonging and purpose in our lives.

Compassion is another essential aspect of giving. When we approach others with kindness and empathy, we create a positive and supportive environment that fosters growth and healing. Compassion helps us connect with others on a deeper level, fostering understanding, forgiveness, and acceptance.

22: THE JOY OF GIVING: THE REWARDS OF GENEROS-ITY AND COMPASSION

However, it is essential to note that giving and compassion should not come at the expense of our own well-being. It is crucial to find a balance between giving to others and taking care of ourselves. We must ensure that we are not sacrificing our own needs and well-being in the process.

One way to ensure this balance is to practice mindful giving. This means being intentional about our giving, considering the impact it will have on both the recipient and ourselves. Mindful giving also means setting boundaries and being clear about our intentions and limitations.

Another important aspect of giving is cultivating a mindset of abundance. This means recognizing that there is enough to go around and that giving does not diminish our own resources. It is a mindset that allows us to approach life with generosity and openness, creating a positive and supportive environment that benefits everyone.

In conclusion, the joy of giving is a powerful and transformative experience that can have a profound impact on our physical, emotional, and mental well-being. It is a practice that fosters compassion, generosity, and connection, creating a sense of purpose and meaning in our lives. By cultivat-

22: THE JOY OF GIVING: THE REWARDS OF GENEROS-ITY AND COMPASSION

ing a mindset of abundance and practicing mindful giving, we can reap the many rewards of generosity and compassion, both for ourselves and for those around us.

23: Overcoming Fear: Finding Courage and Confidence

Fear is an emotion that can hold us back from achieving our full potential. It can stop us from pursuing our dreams, taking risks, and trying new things. Fear can be paralyzing, and it can keep us stuck in a cycle of anxiety and self-doubt.

But fear doesn't have to control us. With the right mindset and strategies, we can overcome our fears and find the courage and confidence to live the life we want. In this chapter, we'll explore the science behind fear and how we can use this knowledge to overcome our fears and achieve our goals.

Understanding Fear

Before we can overcome our fears, we need to understand what fear is and how it affects us. Fear is a natural human emotion that evolved to protect us from danger. When we perceive a threat, our brains activate the fight or flight response, releasing adrenaline and other hormones that prepare us to either fight the threat or run away from it.

While fear can be a useful response in certain situations, such as when we're facing a physical threat, it can also be triggered by perceived threats that are not actually danger-ous. This is known as an irrational fear or phobia, and it can be extremely limiting and debilitating.

For example, a fear of public speaking may not be rational, as speaking in front of a group of people is not actually dan-gerous. However, the fear response can be so strong that it can cause physical symptoms such as sweating, shaking, and nausea, making it difficult to perform the task.

Identifying Your Fears

The first step in overcoming your fears is to identify what they are. This may seem obvious, but sometimes our fears are so ingrained that we're not even aware of them. Take some time to reflect on your life and think about the things that make you feel anxious or uncomfortable.

Some common fears include:

– Fear of failure

– Fear of rejection

– Fear of the unknown

23: OVERCOMING FEAR: FINDING COURAGE AND CONFIDENCE

– Fear of change

– Fear of public speaking

– Fear of heights

– Fear of flying

– Fear of spiders, snakes, or other animals

Once you've identified your fears, it's important to recognize that they're not necessarily rational or based in reality. It's possible to be afraid of something that isn't actually dangerous, or to have a fear that's disproportionate to the level of risk.

Challenging Your Fears

Once you've identified your fears, the next step is to challenge them. This means questioning the assumptions and beliefs that underlie your fear and examining the evidence that supports or contradicts them.

For example, if you have a fear of public speaking, you might examine the belief that you're not a good speaker and that people will judge you negatively. You could then look for evidence that contradicts this belief, such as times when you've given a successful presentation or positive feedback you've received in the past.

Another strategy for challenging your fears is to expose yourself to them in a controlled environment. This is known as exposure therapy, and it involves gradually increasing your exposure to the thing you fear while practicing relaxation techniques to help manage your anxiety.

For example, if you have a fear of flying, you might start by watching videos of airplanes taking off and landing, then progress to sitting in a parked airplane, and eventually taking a short flight.

Building Courage and Confidence

Overcoming your fears takes courage, and building courage and confidence is a process that takes time and effort. Here are some strategies for building courage and confidence:

Take small steps. Start by facing your fears in small, manageable ways. This will help build your confidence and give you the courage to take bigger steps later on.

Practice self-care. Taking care of yourself physically and emotionally can help build resilience and give you the strength to face your fears. This includes getting enough sleep, eating a healthy diet, exercising regularly, and practicing relaxation techniques such as meditation or deep breathing.

Surround yourself with supportive people. Having a strong support system can make all the difference when it comes to overcoming your fears. Surround yourself with people who believe in you and encourage you to take risks and pursue your goals.

Focus on the positive. When you're facing a fear, it's easy to focus on the negative outcomes and potential dangers. Instead, try to focus on the positive aspects of the situation, such as the potential rewards and the personal growth that comes from facing your fears.

Celebrate your successes. When you take steps to overcome your fears, even small ones, it's important to celebrate your successes. This reinforces the positive behavior and helps build your confidence for future challenges.

The Power of Mindset

Ultimately, overcoming your fears requires a mindset shift. It means shifting your focus from the potential risks and negative outcomes to the potential rewards and personal growth that come from facing your fears.

One way to shift your mindset is to reframe your thoughts. This means consciously changing your negative or limiting thoughts into more positive and empowering ones. For example, instead of thinking "I can't do this," try reframing it as "I haven't done this before, but I can learn and grow from the experience."

Another powerful mindset shift is to embrace a growth mindset. This means believing that your abilities and intelligence are not fixed, but can be developed through effort and perseverance. When you embrace a growth mindset, you're more likely to take risks and face challenges, knowing that failure is not a permanent condition but a temporary setback on the road to success.

23: OVERCOMING FEAR: FINDING COURAGE AND CONFIDENCE

Conclusion

Fear is a natural human emotion that can hold us back from achieving our full potential. But with the right mindset and strategies, we can overcome our fears and find the courage and confidence to live the life we want. By identifying our fears, challenging our assumptions, and building courage and confidence, we can unleash our inner joy and achieve enduring happiness.

24: The Role of Acceptance in Achieving Enduring Happiness

Introduction

Happiness is a fundamental human desire, and many people spend their entire lives searching for it. They try different things like material possessions, relationships, careers, and even drugs, but most of these efforts are short-lived and end in disappointment. The reason is that happiness is not something that can be obtained externally. It is an internal state that requires a shift in mindset and a deep understanding of oneself.

One essential component of achieving happiness is acceptance. It is the art of acknowledging reality, both the good and the bad, without judgment or resistance. Acceptance can help us cultivate a sense of inner peace and contentment that leads to lasting happiness. In this chapter, we will explore the role of acceptance in achieving enduring happiness and how we can cultivate it in our lives.

Acceptance Defined

Acceptance is the willingness to experience reality as it is,

without trying to change or control it. It is about acknowledging and embracing the present moment, whether it is
pleasant or not. It involves letting go of the past and future
and focusing on the here and now. Acceptance is not resig-
nation or passivity. It is an active choice to respond to reality with an open mind and heart.

The Importance of Acceptance in Achieving Enduring Happiness

Reducing Stress and Anxiety

One of the primary benefits of acceptance is that it reduces
stress and anxiety. When we resist reality or try to control
it, we create tension and inner conflict. This tension can
manifest physically as stress and mentally as anxiety. Acceptance allows us to let go of this tension and find inner
peace, even in challenging situations.

Improving Relationships

Acceptance is also essential in improving our relationships.
When we accept others as they are, without judgment or criticism, we create a space of openness and understanding.

24: THE ROLE OF ACCEPTANCE IN ACHIEVING ENDURING HAPPINESS

This space allows for authentic connection and intimacy, which can enhance our relationships' quality and longevity.

Enhancing Self-Awareness

Acceptance also enhances self-awareness. When we accept ourselves as we are, with all our flaws and imperfections, we gain insight into our true selves. This insight allows us to grow and develop as individuals, leading to greater self-awareness and personal growth.

Boosting Resilience

Finally, acceptance is crucial in boosting resilience. When we accept reality as it is, we can adapt to change and bounce back from setbacks more easily. This resilience allows us to navigate life's ups and downs with grace and ease.

Cultivating Acceptance in Our Lives

Mindfulness Meditation

One of the most effective ways to cultivate acceptance is through mindfulness meditation. Mindfulness meditation involves bringing our attention to the present moment and observing our thoughts and emotions without judgment or reaction. This practice allows us to develop a sense of inner peace and acceptance, which can carry over into our daily lives.

Self-Compassion

Self-compassion is another powerful tool for cultivating acceptance. Self-compassion involves treating ourselves with kindness and understanding, just as we would treat a friend. This practice allows us to accept ourselves as we are, with all our flaws and imperfections, and cultivate a sense of self-love and acceptance.

Gratitude

Gratitude is also essential in cultivating acceptance. When we focus on what we have rather than what we lack, we create a sense of abundance and contentment. This contentment allows us to accept our current reality and find joy in the present moment.

Mindset Shifts

Finally, cultivating acceptance requires a shift in mindset.

24: THE ROLE OF ACCEPTANCE IN ACHIEVING EN-DURING HAPPINESS

We must learn to see reality as it is, without judgment or resistance. This shift in mindset takes practice and requires a willingness to let go of our ego and embrace humility.

Conclusion

Acceptance is a crucial component of achieving enduring happiness. It allows us to let go of resistance and find inner peace, even in challenging situations. By reducing stress and anxiety, improving relationships, enhancing self-aware-ness, and boosting resilience, acceptance can lead to a more fulfilling and joyful life.

Cultivating acceptance in our lives requires a combination of mindfulness meditation, self-compassion, gratitude, and mindset shifts. It takes practice and dedication to develop a mindset of acceptance, but the rewards are well worth the effort.

As we embrace acceptance, we begin to see the beauty in life's imperfections and find joy in the present moment. We no longer need to chase happiness externally because we have found it within ourselves. Acceptance is the key to un-locking our inner joy and achieving enduring happiness.

25: The Art of Mindful Communication: Enhancing Relationships and Resolving Conflict

As human beings, we have a deep-seated need for connection and relationships with others. Communication is the foundation of all relationships. It is the key to unlocking the doors to meaningful connections, empathy, understanding, and love. However, effective communication is not always easy, and misunderstandings can lead to conflict and damaged relationships.

Mindful communication is a powerful tool that can help us enhance our relationships, resolve conflicts, and achieve enduring happiness. It involves paying attention to our own thoughts, feelings, and reactions while being fully present and attentive to others during conversations. In this chapter, we will explore the art of mindful communication and learn how to use it to create deeper connections, resolve conflicts, and cultivate joy in our relationships.

The Power of Mindful Communication

Mindful communication is not just about listening, it's about being fully present and attentive to the person you're communicating with. It means being open and curious, trying to understand their perspective, and communicating in a way that is respectful and empathetic.

When we communicate mindfully, we become more aware of our own thoughts and emotions, and we learn to express them in a way that is authentic and honest. We also become more attuned to the thoughts and feelings of others, which helps us to respond in a way that is more empathetic and understanding.

One of the biggest benefits of mindful communication is that it can help us to resolve conflicts in a way that is constructive and respectful. When we communicate mindfully, we are less likely to become defensive or aggressive, and we are more likely to be able to find common ground and reach a mutually beneficial solution.

Another benefit of mindful communication is that it can help us to deepen our relationships with others. When we communicate mindfully, we create an environment of trust and understanding, which can help us to build stronger and more meaningful connections with others.

25: THE ART OF MINDFUL COMMUNICATION: ENHANCING RELATIONSHIPS AND RESOLVING CONFLICT

Keys to Mindful Communication

There are several key principles to mindful communication that can help us to become more effective communicators and build stronger relationships with others.

Presence

The first key to mindful communication is presence. Presence means being fully present and attentive to the person you're communicating with. It means putting aside distractions and focusing all of your attention on the person in front of you.

When you're communicating mindfully, you're not just listening to what the other person is saying; you're also paying attention to their body language, tone of voice, and facial expressions. This level of attentiveness allows you to pick up on subtle cues and better understand the person's perspective.

Authenticity

The second key to mindful communication is authenticity. Authenticity means being true to yourself and expressing your thoughts and feelings in a way that is honest and genuine.

When you communicate authentically, you're not trying to be someone you're not or hide your true feelings. Instead, you're being open and vulnerable, sharing your thoughts and emotions in a way that is authentic and true to yourself.

Empathy

The third key to mindful communication is empathy. Empathy means putting yourself in the other person's shoes and trying to understand their perspective.

When you communicate empathetically, you're not just focused on your own needs and desires; you're also considering the other person's needs and desires. This allows you to communicate in a way that is more respectful and compassionate, and it can help to create a deeper sense of understanding and connection.

Respect

The fourth key to mindful communication is respect. Respect means treating the other person with dignity and showing them that you value their thoughts, feelings, and opinions.

When you communicate respectfully, you're not attacking or belittling the other person; you're expressing your thoughts and feelings in a way that is respectful and considerate. This creates a safe space for communication and helps to build trust and understanding.

Non-judgment

The fifth key to mindful communication is non-judgment. Non-judgment means refraining from judging or criticizing the other person's thoughts, feelings, or opinions.

When you communicate without judgment, you're creating an environment of acceptance and understanding. This allows the other person to feel safe and comfortable expressing themselves, which can lead to deeper and more meaningful conversations.

Clarity

The sixth key to mindful communication is clarity. Clarity means expressing your thoughts and feelings in a clear and concise way.

When you communicate with clarity, you're making it easier for the other person to understand your perspective. This can help to prevent misunderstandings and can lead to more effective communication overall.

Active listening

The seventh key to mindful communication is active listening. Active listening means being fully present and engaged in the conversation and actively trying to understand the other person's perspective.

When you listen actively, you're not just waiting for your turn to speak; you're fully engaged in the conversation, asking questions, and seeking to understand the other person's point of view.

Putting Mindful Communication into Practice

Now that we've explored the key principles of mindful communication, let's look at how we can put them into practice in our daily lives.

25: THE ART OF MINDFUL COMMUNICATION: ENHANCING RELATIONSHIPS AND RESOLVING CONFLICT

Practice mindfulness

The first step to practicing mindful communication is to practice mindfulness. Mindfulness is the practice of being fully present and attentive to the present moment. It involves paying attention to your thoughts, emotions, and physical sensations without judgment.

Practicing mindfulness can help you become more aware of your own thoughts and emotions, which can make it easier to communicate authentically and empathetically with others.

Listen actively

The second step to practicing mindful communication is to listen actively. Active listening involves paying attention to the other person's words, tone of voice, and body language. It means asking questions and seeking to understand the other person's perspective.

When you listen actively, you create a space for the other person to express themselves fully, which can lead to deeper and more meaningful conversations.

25: THE ART OF MINDFUL COMMUNICATION: ENHANCING RELATIONSHIPS AND RESOLVING CONFLICT

Speak authentically

The third step to practicing mindful communication is to speak authentically. Authentic communication means expressing your thoughts and feelings in a way that is honest and true to yourself.

When you speak authentically, you create a space for others to do the same. This can help to build trust and understanding in your relationships.

Show empathy

The fourth step to practicing mindful communication is to show empathy. Empathy means putting yourself in the other person's shoes and trying to understand their perspective.

When you show empathy, you create a space for the other person to feel heard and understood. This can help to build deeper connections and stronger relationships.

Practice non-judgment

The fifth step to practicing mindful communication is to

practice non-judgment. Non-judgment means refraining
from judging or criticizing the other person's thoughts, feelings, or opinions.

When you practice non-judgment, you create a space for the
other person to express themselves without fear of judgment. This can lead to more open and honest communication.

Be respectful

The sixth step to practicing mindful communication is to be
respectful. Respect means treating the other person with
dignity and showing them that you value their thoughts,
feelings, and opinions.

When you communicate respectfully, you create a space for
the other person to feel safe and heard. This can help to
build trust and understanding in your relationships.

Seek clarity

The seventh step to practicing mindful communication is to
seek clarity. Clarity means expressing your thoughts and
feelings in a clear and concise way.

25: THE ART OF MINDFUL COMMUNICATION: ENHANCING RELATIONSHIPS AND RESOLVING CONFLICT

When you seek clarity, you make it easier for the other person to understand your perspective. This can help to prevent misunderstandings and can lead to more effective communication overall.

26: The Importance of Boundaries: Setting Limits for Healthy Relationships

When it comes to relationships, boundaries play a crucial role in maintaining a healthy dynamic. Yet, they are often overlooked or even dismissed as unnecessary. However, setting and respecting boundaries can be a game-changer in achieving euphoria and enduring happiness in all types of relationships, including romantic, familial, and even professional.

Firstly, what are boundaries? Boundaries are the guidelines that we set for ourselves in our interactions with others. They define what we are comfortable with and what we are not. They are not about controlling other people but about protecting ourselves and our well-being. Boundaries can be physical, emotional, or intellectual, and they can change over time as we grow and evolve.

Without boundaries, we can become easily overwhelmed and drained in our relationships. For instance, we might find ourselves giving more than we receive, sacrificing our own needs and desires to please others, or allowing others to treat us in a way that is not respectful or healthy. Boundaries help us to draw the line between what we are willing to accept and what we are not, thereby enabling us to have more control over our lives and interactions.

Moreover, boundaries are crucial for fostering a sense of self-respect and self-worth. When we have clear boundaries, we communicate to others that we value and prioritize ourselves. This can be a powerful way of attracting people who are also respectful and supportive of us. Conversely, when we don't have clear boundaries, we may attract people who take advantage of us or who do not respect our needs and boundaries. In such cases, we may find ourselves feeling used, unappreciated, or even resentful towards those we are in a relationship with.

That said, setting boundaries is not always easy. It can be challenging to communicate our needs and preferences to others, especially if we fear that we will be judged or rejected. It can also be challenging to maintain our boundaries, especially if we are used to people-pleasing or are afraid of conflict. However, with practice and persistence, setting and maintaining boundaries can become easier and more natural.

Here are some strategies for setting and maintaining healthy boundaries:

Get clear on your needs and preferences: Before you can set boundaries, you need to know what your needs and preferences are. Take some time to reflect on what makes you feel comfortable and uncomfortable in your relationships. This might include things like how much time you want to spend with someone, what topics you do not want to discuss, or what behaviors you will not tolerate.

Communicate your boundaries clearly and assertively: Once you know what your boundaries are, it's essential to communicate them clearly and assertively to others. This means expressing your needs and preferences in a direct and respectful manner. Avoid being vague or passive-aggressive, as this can create confusion and frustration.

Practice self-care: Setting and maintaining boundaries can be emotionally draining, so it's essential to prioritize self-care. This might include taking time for yourself, engaging in activities that make you feel happy and fulfilled, or seeking support from friends, family, or a therapist.

Respect other people's boundaries: Just as you have the right to set boundaries, so do others. Respect their boundaries, even if they are different from yours. This means listening to their needs and preferences and not pressuring them to do something they are not comfortable with.

Be open to negotiation: Sometimes, boundaries can conflict with others' needs and preferences. In such cases, it's essential to be open to negotiation and compromise. This might involve finding a middle ground that is acceptable to both parties or finding alternative ways of meeting each other's needs.

In conclusion, setting and maintaining boundaries is an essential aspect of healthy relationships. It enables us to prioritize our needs and well-being while also respecting others' needs and preferences.

27: The Benefits of Solitude: Finding Peace and Clarity in Alone Time

As human beings, we are wired for social interaction. We thrive in the company of others, and our social connections play a vital role in our overall well-being. However, amidst the constant stimulation and noise of modern-day living, we often overlook the importance of solitude. Solitude refers to the state of being alone, away from the company of others. For many of us, the thought of being alone can be unsettling, and we associate it with loneliness and isolation. However, solitude can be a powerful tool in achieving enduring happiness and personal growth. In this chapter, we will explore the benefits of solitude, and how you can use it to find peace, clarity, and contentment in your life.

One of the most significant benefits of solitude is that it allows us to disconnect from the external noise and distractions of the world. In our fast-paced, technology-driven society, we are bombarded with information, stimuli, and demands from every direction. Our attention is constantly divided, and our minds are always racing. Taking time out for solitude can help us to clear our minds, refocus our attention, and recharge our batteries. It provides an opportunity to slow down, reflect, and be present in the moment.

In addition to providing a respite from external distractions, solitude can also help us to tune in to our internal landscape. When we are alone, we have the space and time to listen to our inner voice, to connect with our intuition, and to explore our thoughts and feelings. This can be a powerful tool for self-discovery, personal growth, and creativity. By spending time in solitude, we can learn more about ourselves, our values, and our passions, and gain a deeper understanding of our purpose and direction in life.

Another benefit of solitude is that it can help us to cultivate a sense of inner peace and tranquility. When we are alone, we have the freedom to engage in activities that bring us joy and relaxation, such as reading, meditating, or taking a leisurely walk in nature. These activities can help us to quiet our minds, reduce stress and anxiety, and promote a sense of well-being. Moreover, solitude can provide us with the opportunity to engage in spiritual practices, such as prayer or contemplation, which can deepen our connection with the divine and foster a sense of inner calm and serenity.

27: THE BENEFITS OF SOLITUDE: FINDING PEACE AND CLARITY IN ALONE TIME

While solitude may seem like a solitary pursuit, it can also have positive effects on our relationships with others. When we take time out for solitude, we are better able to connect with ourselves, which in turn can help us to connect more authentically with others. By developing a strong sense of self-awareness and self-esteem through solitude, we are more likely to engage in healthy relationships that are based on mutual respect, trust, and understanding. Additionally, when we take time out for solitude, we can return to our relationships feeling more energized, refreshed, and engaged, which can have a positive impact on the quality of our interactions with others.

Despite the many benefits of solitude, many people find it difficult to embrace. We live in a culture that celebrates extroversion, socializing, and being constantly connected. The idea of being alone can be seen as a sign of weakness or inadequacy, and we may fear being judged or rejected by others if we choose to spend time in solitude. However, it's important to remember that solitude is not a sign of weakness, but rather a sign of strength and self-awareness. It takes courage to be alone with oneself, to confront our fears and vulnerabilities, and to explore our inner landscape. By embracing solitude, we can develop a deeper sense of self-acceptance, self-love, and self-worth, which can ultimately lead to greater happiness and fulfillment in life.

So, how can we cultivate solitude in our lives and reap its many benefits? The first step is to make time for it. Set aside dedicated periods of alone time in your schedule, whether it's a few minutes each day, an hour once a week, or a weekend retreat every few months. It's important to prioritize solitude as a valuable and necessary part of your self-care routine.

Next, embrace the idea of being alone. Rather than viewing it as a negative experience, try to reframe your mindset and see it as an opportunity for growth and self-discovery. Think of it as a chance to recharge your batteries, connect with your inner self, and cultivate a sense of peace and clarity.

When you are in solitude, engage in activities that bring you joy and relaxation. This could be anything from taking a bubble bath, practicing yoga, or listening to music to writing in a journal, drawing, or simply sitting quietly and reflecting. The key is to engage in activities that nourish your mind, body, and spirit and promote a sense of inner peace and tranquility.

Finally, practice self-compassion and self-care. If you find yourself feeling anxious or uncomfortable in solitude, remember that this is a normal part of the process. Allow yourself to feel your emotions and be gentle with yourself. Take care of your basic needs, such as getting enough sleep, eating well, and exercising regularly. By prioritizing your own well-being, you can cultivate a deeper sense of self-love and self-acceptance, which can ultimately lead to greater happiness and fulfillment in life.

In conclusion, solitude is a powerful tool for achieving enduring happiness and personal growth. By disconnecting from external distractions and tuning in to our inner selves, we can cultivate a sense of peace, clarity, and contentment in our lives. Despite societal pressures to be constantly connected and engaged, it's important to prioritize solitude as a valuable and necessary part of our self-care routine. So, take a deep breath, unplug from the world, and embrace the beauty and benefits of solitude.

28: The Power of Nature: Finding Joy and Healing in the Great Outdoors

As humans, we have a deep-rooted connection with nature. We have evolved over millions of years in harmony with the natural world, and our modern lifestyles often keep us disconnected from it. Spending time in nature has a powerful impact on our physical and mental wellbeing, and it is a critical component of achieving enduring happiness.

In this chapter, we will explore the benefits of spending time in nature, the science behind it, and how to incorporate it into your daily life. Whether you are an outdoor enthusiast or a city dweller, this chapter will provide you with the tools to unleash your inner joy and find healing in the great outdoors.

The Healing Power of Nature

There is no denying that nature has a profound impact on our wellbeing. From reducing stress to improving our cognitive function, spending time in nature has a multitude of benefits. Studies have shown that spending just 20 minutes in nature can significantly reduce cortisol levels, our body's stress hormone. Additionally, exposure to nature has been linked to improved mood, lower blood pressure, and decreased symptoms of anxiety and depression.

One study conducted in Japan found that participants who spent time walking in the forest had lower levels of cortisol, lower blood pressure, and lower heart rate compared to those who walked in a city environment. The participants who spent time in the forest also reported feeling more relaxed and refreshed than those who walked in the city.

The benefits of nature are not just limited to our physical health. Nature has a profound impact on our mental well-being as well. Studies have shown that spending time in nature can improve our cognitive function, creativity, and attention span. Additionally, exposure to nature has been linked to improved self-esteem and reduced symptoms of depression.

Incorporating Nature into Your Daily Life

Now that we understand the benefits of spending time in nature let's explore how to incorporate it into our daily lives. For those who live in urban areas, finding nature can be a challenge, but it's not impossible. Here are some tips to incorporate nature into your daily routine:

Take a walk in a nearby park or nature reserve. Even a short walk can have a significant impact on your physical and mental wellbeing.

Start a garden, no matter how small. Gardening is a great way to connect with nature and get some exercise.

Bring nature inside. Adding plants to your home or workspace can have a calming effect and improve air quality.

Find a local community garden or urban farm. Many cities have community gardens where you can get involved in growing your food and connect with like-minded people.

Take up outdoor hobbies such as birdwatching, fishing, or hiking. These activities not only connect you with nature but also provide an opportunity to exercise and explore new places.

For those who live in more rural areas, nature is often readily available, but it can still be challenging to make time for it. Here are some tips to incorporate nature into your daily routine:

Take a daily walk in nature. Even a short walk can have a significant impact on your physical and mental wellbeing.

Practice mindfulness in nature. Take time to notice the sounds, smells, and sensations around you, and let go of any stress or worries.

Plan regular camping or hiking trips. These trips not only provide an opportunity to connect with nature but also to disconnect from technology and spend time with loved ones.

Volunteer for local conservation efforts. Contributing to the preservation of nature is not only rewarding but also provides an opportunity to connect with like-minded people and learn more about the natural world.

Incorporate nature into your exercise routine. Try outdoor yoga, running, or cycling to enjoy the benefits of nature while getting some exercise.

The Power of Mindset Shifts

28: THE POWER OF NATURE: FINDING JOY AND HEALING IN THE GREAT OUTDOORS

Incorporating nature into your daily life is not only about the physical and mental benefits but also about shifting your mindset. It's about recognizing the importance of nature in our lives and making a conscious effort to prioritize it. Here are some mindset shifts to help you connect with nature on a deeper level:

Gratitude: Practice gratitude for the natural world and all the benefits it provides. Take time to appreciate the beauty of nature and the peace it brings.

Connection: Recognize that we are all connected to the natural world, and our actions have a significant impact on the environment. Take responsibility for your actions and make an effort to reduce your carbon footprint.

Awareness: Become more aware of your surroundings and the impact nature has on your physical and mental well-being. Take time to notice the sounds, smells, and sensations around you, and let go of any stress or worries.

Respect: Treat nature with respect and recognize that it is not here for our exploitation but for our enjoyment and sustenance. Take care not to litter or damage natural habit-

28: THE POWER OF NATURE: FINDING JOY AND HEALING IN THE GREAT OUTDOORS

ats.

Mindfulness: Practice mindfulness in nature, focusing on the present moment and letting go of any distractions or stressors. Take time to breathe deeply and soak in the natural world around you.

The Bottom Line

Nature has a powerful impact on our physical and mental wellbeing, and it is a critical component of achieving enduring happiness. By incorporating nature into our daily lives and shifting our mindset, we can connect with the natural world on a deeper level and unleash our inner joy.

Whether you live in an urban or rural area, there are ways to incorporate nature into your daily routine. Take a walk in a nearby park, start a garden, or take up outdoor hobbies such as hiking or birdwatching. Whatever your approach, make a conscious effort to prioritize nature in your life, and you will reap the benefits of improved physical and mental wellbeing.

In conclusion, the power of nature is undeniable, and it is

up to us to harness its healing potential. By spending time in nature, incorporating it into our daily lives, and shifting our mindset, we can find joy and healing in the great outdoors. So, go ahead, take a deep breath, and immerse yourself in the beauty of the natural world around you.

29: The Joy of Adventure: Exploring and Experiencing New Things

There is something undeniably thrilling about trying new things. Whether it's traveling to a new place, trying a new food, or taking up a new hobby, the experience of exploring the unknown can be both exhilarating and deeply fulfilling. In this chapter, we'll explore the science behind why trying new things can bring us such joy, as well as practical strategies for incorporating more adventure into our lives.

The Science of Adventure

To understand why trying new things can be so rewarding, it's helpful to first take a look at what's happening in our brains. When we experience something novel or exciting, our brains release a chemical called dopamine. This neurotransmitter is responsible for feelings of pleasure, motivation, and reward, and it plays a crucial role in our ability to learn and adapt to new situations.

In addition to dopamine, trying new things can also stimulate other parts of the brain, such as the prefrontal cortex and the hippocampus. These regions are involved in cognitive processing, memory, and learning, and they can become stronger and more efficient with repeated exposure to new experiences.

But it's not just our brains that benefit from trying new things. Adventure and exploration can also have profound effects on our mental and emotional well-being. Research has shown that people who engage in novel and challenging activities are more likely to experience positive emotions like excitement, joy, and awe. They may also be more resilient in the face of adversity, better able to cope with stress, and less likely to experience symptoms of depression and anxiety.

In short, trying new things can be a powerful way to tap into our innate capacity for joy and fulfillment. So how can we incorporate more adventure into our lives?

Practical Strategies for Adventure

One of the easiest ways to try new things is to simply make a conscious effort to seek out novel experiences. This might mean trying a new restaurant or cuisine, taking up a new hobby or sport, or traveling to a new destination.

29: THE JOY OF ADVENTURE: EXPLORING AND EX-PERIENCING NEW THINGS

But it's not enough to just try something new once and then move on. To truly reap the benefits of adventure, we need to make a habit of seeking out new experiences and pushing ourselves outside of our comfort zones.

Here are a few strategies for incorporating more adventure into your life:

Set a goal to try something new every week, whether it's a new food, activity, or experience. Make it a priority to seek out opportunities to learn and explore.

Step outside of your comfort zone. Challenge yourself to try something that feels intimidating or unfamiliar. This could be anything from skydiving to learning a new language to attending a social event where you don't know anyone.

Embrace spontaneity. Sometimes the best adventures are the ones that happen on a whim. Say yes to unexpected invitations and be open to trying something new at a moment's notice.

Travel to new places. Whether it's a weekend road trip or an international excursion, travel is one of the best ways to experience new cultures, foods, and activities.

Take up a new hobby or sport. Whether it's painting, rock climbing, or salsa dancing, finding a new passion can be a great way to challenge yourself and discover new parts of yourself.

The Joy of Adventure

Ultimately, the key to experiencing the joy of adventure is to approach life with an open mind and a willingness to take risks. When we embrace the unknown and allow ourselves to be vulnerable to new experiences, we tap into a deep well of joy and fulfillment that can transform our lives.

So don't be afraid to try new things, to explore uncharted territory, and to push yourself outside of your comfort zone. Life is an adventure, and the more we embrace it, the richer and more rewarding our experiences will be.

30: The Role of Humor in Achieving Euphoria: Finding Laughter and Joy in Everyday Life

Laughter is often referred to as the best medicine. It's a universal language that can bridge cultural and language barriers, and it has the power to connect people in ways that words alone cannot. But did you know that laughter and humor also play a vital role in achieving euphoria? In this chapter, we'll explore the science behind humor and how it can help us find joy and happiness in our everyday lives.

To understand the role of humor in achieving euphoria, we need to first understand what laughter is and why we laugh. Laughter is a complex physiological response that involves a combination of facial expressions, vocalizations, and body movements. It's an innate behavior that's shared by all humans, and it's often triggered by humorous or absurd situations.

But laughter is more than just a response to humor. Studies have shown that laughter can have a range of positive effects on both our physical and mental health. Laughter has been found to boost the immune system, lower blood pressure, reduce stress hormones, and release endorphins, which are the body's natural painkillers and mood enhancers.

So, how can we incorporate humor into our lives to achieve euphoria? The good news is that there are many ways to find laughter and joy in everyday life. Here are some science-backed strategies and mindset shifts that can help:

Embrace the Absurd: One of the keys to finding humor in everyday life is to embrace the absurd. Life is full of unexpected twists and turns, and sometimes the best way to deal with these situations is to find the humor in them. Try to see the funny side of things, even when they don't go according to plan.

Surround Yourself with Humor: Another way to incorporate humor into your life is to surround yourself with people and things that make you laugh. Spend time with friends who have a good sense of humor, watch comedies or funny YouTube videos, or read humorous books or articles.

Practice Self-Deprecation: While it's important to take ourselves seriously, it's also important to be able to laugh at ourselves. Practice self-deprecating humor, where you make fun of yourself in a light-hearted way. Not only will it help you find humor in your own flaws and mistakes, but it will also help others feel more comfortable around you.

Find Humor in Stressful Situations: When life gets stressful, it can be difficult to find humor in anything. But studies have shown that finding humor in stressful situations can actually help us cope better. Try to find the humor in the situation, even if it's just a small, silly thing. It can help you feel more relaxed and better able to handle the stress.

Incorporate Playfulness into Your Life: Playfulness is a key component of humor and can help us find joy and happiness in everyday life. Incorporate playful activities into your day, such as playing with your pets, dancing around your living room, or playing silly games with friends.

Practice Gratitude: Gratitude is another important component of achieving euphoria. When we focus on the positive things in our lives, we're more likely to find joy and happiness. Try keeping a gratitude journal where you write down things you're thankful for each day. It can help shift your mindset towards a more positive outlook.

30: THE ROLE OF HUMOR IN ACHIEVING EUPHORIA: FINDING LAUGHTER AND JOY IN EVERYDAY LIFE

Incorporating humor and laughter into our lives may seem like a small thing, but it can have a big impact on our overall happiness and wellbeing. By embracing the absurd, surrounding ourselves with humor, practicing self-deprecation, finding humor in stressful situations, incorporating playfulness, and practicing gratitude, we can achieve enduring happiness and unleash our inner joy. So, go ahead and laugh - it's good for you!

31: The Importance of Perspective: Changing Your Outlook for Lasting Happiness

The human experience is full of ups and downs, and it is all too easy to become bogged down by negative emotions and events. However, there is a way to break free from this cycle and achieve lasting happiness: by changing your perspective. By altering the way you view the world around you, you can unlock a state of euphoria that will bring you joy and fulfillment for years to come.

In this chapter, we will explore the importance of perspective and provide you with science-backed strategies and life-changing mindset shifts that will help you unleash your inner joy and achieve enduring happiness.

The Power of Perspective

Perspective refers to the way you view the world around you. It is influenced by your beliefs, values, experiences, and culture. Your perspective shapes your thoughts, emotions, and actions, and it can either help you or hinder you in achieving your goals and experiencing happiness.

For example, imagine that you are stuck in traffic on your way to an important meeting. Your perspective could be negative, focusing on the inconvenience, frustration, and potential consequences of being late. Alternatively, your perspective could be positive, recognizing that you have extra time to review your notes, listen to an audiobook, or simply enjoy the scenery around you.

The difference between these two perspectives may seem small, but it can have a significant impact on your emotional state and overall well-being. Studies have shown that people who adopt a positive perspective are more resilient, less stressed, and happier than those who adopt a negative perspective. They are also more likely to succeed in their personal and professional endeavors.

Changing Your Perspective for Lasting Happiness

Fortunately, your perspective is not set in stone. With practice and intention, you can change the way you view the world and unlock a state of euphoria that will bring you lasting happiness. Here are some science-backed strategies and mindset shifts to help you get started:

31: THE IMPORTANCE OF PERSPECTIVE: CHANGING YOUR OUTLOOK FOR LASTING HAPPINESS

Practice Gratitude

Gratitude is a powerful tool for changing your perspective. It involves focusing on the positive aspects of your life and appreciating what you have, rather than dwelling on what you lack or what is going wrong. Research has shown that practicing gratitude can increase happiness, improve relationships, and boost resilience.

To practice gratitude, take a few minutes each day to reflect on the things you are grateful for. You can write them down in a journal, say them out loud, or simply think about them. Focus on both big and small things, such as your health, your relationships, your accomplishments, or a beautiful sunset.

Challenge Your Negative Thoughts

Negative thoughts can be a major roadblock to happiness. They can lead to feelings of anxiety, depression, and hopelessness, and can prevent you from taking action towards your goals. To change your perspective, you need to challenge these negative thoughts and replace them with more positive, realistic ones.

To do this, start by identifying your negative thoughts. Write them down and ask yourself whether they are true, whether they are helpful, and whether there is evidence to support them. Then, try to reframe them in a more positive or realistic way. For example, instead of thinking "I'll never be able to do this," try "This is a challenge, but I can break it down into smaller steps and make progress."

Cultivate Mindfulness

Mindfulness is the practice of being present in the moment, without judgment or distraction. It can help you tune into your thoughts and emotions, and become more aware of your perspective. Research has shown that mindfulness can reduce stress, improve mood, and increase well-being.

To cultivate mindfulness, try to set aside a few minutes each day to focus on your breath and the sensations in your body. You can also try mindfulness exercises such as body scans, mindful walking, or loving-kindness meditation. The key is to be present in the moment and observe your thoughts and emotions without judgment or attachment.

Embrace a Growth Mindset

31: THE IMPORTANCE OF PERSPECTIVE: CHANGING YOUR OUTLOOK FOR LASTING HAPPINESS

A growth mindset is the belief that you can develop your abilities and talents through hard work and perseverance. It is a powerful perspective that can help you overcome obstacles, learn from failure, and achieve your goals. In contrast, a fixed mindset is the belief that your abilities and talents are fixed and cannot be changed.

To embrace a growth mindset, start by identifying your fixed beliefs about yourself and your abilities. Then, challenge these beliefs by asking yourself whether they are really true, and whether they are helpful or limiting. Finally, adopt a growth mindset by focusing on learning and improvement, setting goals that challenge you, and embracing failure as a natural part of the learning process.

Practice Self-Compassion

Self-compassion is the practice of treating yourself with kindness, care, and understanding, especially in the face of failure or adversity. It involves recognizing that you are human, imperfect, and deserving of love and compassion, just like everyone else. Research has shown that self-compassion can reduce stress, improve well-being, and increase resilience.

31: THE IMPORTANCE OF PERSPECTIVE: CHANGING YOUR OUTLOOK FOR LASTING HAPPINESS

To practice self-compassion, start by becoming aware of your self-talk and how you treat yourself when things go wrong. Instead of criticizing or berating yourself, try to offer yourself the same kindness and understanding that you would offer a friend. You can also try self-compassion exercises such as writing a letter to yourself, imagining yourself as a compassionate friend, or practicing self-care.

The Bottom Line

Changing your perspective is a powerful way to achieve lasting happiness and unleash your inner joy. By practicing gratitude, challenging your negative thoughts, cultivating mindfulness, embracing a growth mindset, and practicing self-compassion, you can shift your perspective and experience the world in a more positive, fulfilling way. It takes practice and effort, but the rewards are well worth it. Start today and unleash your inner euphoria!

32: The Benefits of Journaling: Reflection and Self-Discovery

Introduction

Journaling is a powerful tool that can help individuals achieve personal growth and self-discovery. Writing down one's thoughts, feelings, and experiences can provide a deeper understanding of oneself and their surroundings. Journaling is a practice that has been around for centuries, and many famous writers, artists, and thinkers have kept journals to document their lives and gain insights into their creative processes.

In this chapter, we will explore the benefits of journaling and how it can help you achieve euphoria, the state of enduring happiness. We will also provide some science-backed strategies and life-changing mindset shifts to help you get the most out of your journaling practice.

The Benefits of Journaling

Reflection and Self-Discovery

Journaling allows you to reflect on your thoughts, feelings, and experiences. By writing them down, you can gain a deeper understanding of yourself and your surroundings. You can also identify patterns in your behavior and thought processes that may be hindering your personal growth.

Emotional Release

Journaling can be a cathartic experience, allowing you to release pent-up emotions and feelings. Writing down your emotions can help you process them and work through them in a healthy way. It can also help you identify triggers that may be causing emotional distress and find ways to manage them.

Improved Mental Health

Studies have shown that journaling can have a positive impact on mental health. It can help reduce symptoms of depression and anxiety, improve self-esteem, and provide a sense of control over one's life. Writing about traumatic experiences can also be beneficial in the healing process.

Increased Creativity

Journaling can be a great way to spark creativity. Writing down ideas, thoughts, and inspirations can help you develop them further and turn them into something tangible. It can also help you explore new ideas and ways of thinking.

Improved Memory

Journaling can also improve memory. Writing down important events, experiences, and information can help you retain them better. It can also help you recall past events and experiences in more detail.

Science-Backed Strategies for Journaling

Set Aside Time

Set aside time each day to journal. It can be in the morning, at night, or during lunch. The important thing is to make it a habit and stick to it. Even just 10-15 minutes a day can make a big difference.

Write Freely

Write freely without worrying about grammar or spelling. The goal is to get your thoughts and feelings down on paper, not to create a masterpiece. This can help you be more honest and authentic in your writing.

Focus on the Positive

Focus on the positive in your journaling. Write about what you are grateful for, your accomplishments, and things that bring you joy. This can help shift your mindset towards positivity and increase feelings of happiness.

Use Prompts

Use prompts to help guide your writing. Prompts can be anything from a single word to a question or sentence. They can help you explore new ideas and ways of thinking.

Re-Read and Reflect

Re-read your journal entries and reflect on them. This can help you identify patterns in your behavior and thought processes. It can also provide insights into your personal growth and self-discovery.

Life-Changing Mindset Shifts for Journaling

Let Go of Perfectionism

Let go of the idea of perfectionism in your journaling. It's not about creating the perfect entry, but about being honest and authentic in your writing. Embrace imperfection and let your thoughts and feelings flow freely.

Embrace Vulnerability

Embrace vulnerability in your journaling. Write about your fears, insecurities, and struggles. This can help you process them and work through them in a healthy way. It can also help you connect with others on a deeper level, as vulnerability is often a shared experience.

Practice Self-Compassion

Practice self-compassion in your journaling. Be kind and gentle with yourself, even when writing about difficult experiences or emotions. Remember that self-compassion is a key component of self-care and can help promote feelings of happiness and well-being.

Emphasize Progress Over Perfection

Emphasize progress over perfection in your journaling. Focus on the positive changes you are making in your life, rather than on the things you still need to work on. Celebrate your accomplishments and the steps you are taking towards achieving your goals.

Cultivate Gratitude

Cultivate gratitude in your journaling. Write about the things you are grateful for, no matter how small or insignificant they may seem. This can help shift your mindset towards positivity and increase feelings of happiness and contentment.

Conclusion

Journaling is a powerful tool that can help you achieve personal growth, self-discovery, and euphoria. By reflecting on your thoughts, feelings, and experiences, you can gain a deeper understanding of yourself and your surroundings. With science-backed strategies and life-changing mindset shifts, you can get the most out of your journaling practice and unleash your inner joy. So pick up a pen and start writing, and watch as your life transforms before your very eyes.

33: The Joy of Learning: Embracing Lifelong Education and Growth

Introduction

When was the last time you learned something new? Can you recall the feeling of accomplishment and fulfillment that accompanied that experience? Learning is a crucial component of our lives, and it plays an essential role in our well-being and happiness. In this chapter, we will delve into the science of learning and explore how embracing lifelong education and growth can lead to euphoria and lasting happiness.

The Science of Learning

Learning is a fundamental aspect of human development. It is the process of acquiring knowledge, skills, and attitudes through various methods, including observation, experience, and instruction. The science of learning examines how we learn, retain, and recall information and how we can optimize these processes.

There are two primary types of learning: explicit and implicit. Explicit learning involves consciously acquiring knowledge or skills through instruction, practice, or study. Implicit learning, on the other hand, is the unconscious acquisition of knowledge or skills through experience, observation, or intuition.

Research has shown that explicit learning can be enhanced by various strategies, including active participation, repetition, feedback, and contextual learning. Implicit learning, on the other hand, is influenced by factors such as attention, motivation, and prior experience.

The Benefits of Lifelong Learning

Learning does not stop after we finish our formal education. In fact, lifelong learning is essential for our personal and professional growth, and it has numerous benefits for our mental, emotional, and physical health.

Increased Mental Stimulation

Learning provides mental stimulation, which is vital for our cognitive health. Engaging in challenging mental activities, such as learning a new language or taking up a musical instrument, can improve brain function and delay cognitive decline.

Improved Self-Esteem

Learning and mastering a new skill can boost our self-esteem and sense of accomplishment. This, in turn, can lead to a more positive outlook on life and increased confidence.

Enhanced Creativity

Learning exposes us to new ideas and perspectives, which can spark our creativity and inspire us to think outside the box. This can lead to innovative solutions and breakthrough ideas in various aspects of our lives.

Career Advancement

Continuous learning and professional development can enhance our skills and knowledge, making us more competitive in the job market. This can lead to career advancement, increased job satisfaction, and higher earning potential.

Improved Health and Well-Being

33: THE JOY OF LEARNING: EMBRACING LIFELONG EDUCATION AND GROWTH

Learning has been linked to improved mental and emotional health, as well as physical health. Engaging in intellectually stimulating activities has been shown to reduce the risk of age-related diseases such as dementia, Alzheimer's, and Parkinson's.

Strategies for Lifelong Learning

Now that we have established the importance of lifelong learning, let us explore some strategies for implementing this mindset into our daily lives.

Embrace Curiosity

Curiosity is the driving force behind learning. It is the desire to explore, discover, and understand the world around us. Embracing curiosity means being open to new experiences, asking questions, and seeking out knowledge and information.

Set Goals

Setting goals is a powerful tool for motivation and achievement. When we set goals for our learning, we are more likely to stay committed and focused on our objectives. It is essential to set realistic and specific goals that are challenging but achievable.

Create a Learning Plan

Creating a learning plan can help us structure our learning and ensure that we are making progress towards our goals. A learning plan should include specific objectives, timelines, and resources, such as books, courses, or mentors.

Find a Community

Learning can be a solitary activity, but it does not have to be. Finding a community of like-minded individuals can provide support, encouragement, and accountability. This can be achieved through online forums, social media groups, or in-person meetups.

Embrace Failure

Learning involves making mistakes and experiencing failures. It is crucial to embrace failure as a natural part of the learning process and use it as an opportunity to learn and grow. Instead of giving up, we should analyze our mistakes, identify areas for improvement, and try again.

33: THE JOY OF LEARNING: EMBRACING LIFELONG EDUCATION AND GROWTH

Practice Consistently

Consistency is key to achieving long-term success in learning. It is better to practice for short periods consistently than to cram for long hours sporadically. Regular practice helps to reinforce learning and develop new skills and habits.

Explore Different Learning Methods

Everyone learns differently, and it is essential to find a learning method that works for us. Some people learn best through reading, while others prefer visual aids or hands-on activities. Exploring different learning methods can help us identify what works best for us and enhance our learning experience.

Conclusion

Learning is a lifelong journey that provides numerous benefits for our personal and professional growth, as well as our mental, emotional, and physical health. Embracing lifelong education and growth can lead to euphoria and lasting happiness. By embracing curiosity, setting goals, creating a learning plan, finding a community, embracing failure, practicing consistently, and exploring different learning methods, we can unlock our full potential and achieve enduring happiness through the joy of learning.

34: Overcoming Perfectionism: Embracing Imperfection for Greater Happiness

Introduction:

Perfectionism can be a double-edged sword. On one hand, it can drive us to achieve great things, pushing us to be our best selves and excel in our pursuits. On the other hand, it can also be a source of stress, anxiety, and self-doubt. When we strive for perfection, we set ourselves up for failure. We create unrealistic expectations that we can never meet, and when we inevitably fall short, we feel like we've let ourselves down.

In this chapter, we'll explore the concept of perfectionism, its negative effects on our well-being, and the science-backed strategies and mindset shifts we can use to overcome it and embrace imperfection for greater happiness.

What is Perfectionism?

Perfectionism is a personality trait characterized by a person's striving for flawlessness and setting excessively high performance standards, accompanied by overly critical self-evaluations and concerns regarding others' evaluations. It is a tendency to set extremely high standards for oneself and others, and to feel like one is failing if those standards are not met. It can manifest in different areas of life, including work, relationships, appearance, and even hobbies.

Perfectionism is often viewed as a positive attribute, associated with high achievement and success. However, research has shown that it can also be a source of stress, anxiety, and depression, leading to burnout and reduced life satisfaction.

Negative Effects of Perfectionism:

Perfectionism can have negative effects on various aspects of our lives, including our mental health, physical health, and relationships.

Mental Health:

Perfectionism is strongly associated with anxiety and depression. Individuals with perfectionistic tendencies often experience high levels of stress and worry about their performance, which can lead to burnout and reduced life satisfaction.

34: OVERCOMING PERFECTIONISM: EMBRACING IM-PERFECTION FOR GREATER HAPPINESS

Physical Health:

Perfectionism is also linked to physical health problems such as headaches, digestive issues, and insomnia. It can also lead to unhealthy behaviors such as overeating, substance abuse, and self-harm.

Relationships:

Perfectionism can negatively impact our relationships with others. When we hold ourselves and others to impossibly high standards, we set ourselves up for disappointment and conflict. Our relationships become strained, as we struggle to maintain unrealistic expectations.

Overcoming Perfectionism:

Overcoming perfectionism is not easy, but it is possible. The following are science-backed strategies and mindset shifts that can help us embrace imperfection for greater happiness.

Recognize and Challenge Your Inner Critic:

The first step in overcoming perfectionism is to recognize

and challenge your inner critic. This voice in your head that tells you that you're not good enough or that you'll never measure up to your own expectations can be incredibly powerful. However, it's important to remember that this voice is not necessarily a reflection of reality.

When you hear your inner critic, take a moment to challenge its validity. Ask yourself, "Is this really true?" and "What evidence do I have to support this belief?" By questioning your inner critic, you can begin to see it for what it is – a self-imposed set of standards that may not be based in reality.

Practice Self-Compassion:

Self-compassion is the act of treating yourself with the same kindness, concern, and understanding that you would offer to a good friend. It involves acknowledging your own suffering and offering yourself comfort and support.

Practicing self-compassion can help you overcome perfectionism by allowing you to see your mistakes and flaws as part of the human experience. When you make a mistake or fall short of your expectations, instead of berating yourself, offer yourself kindness and understanding.

Set Realistic Goals:

Setting realistic goals is an important part of overcoming perfectionism. Instead of striving for perfection, set achievable goals that are challenging but attainable.

When setting goals, focus on the process rather than the outcome. For example, instead of setting a goal to win a competition, set a goal to train consistently and improve your skills. This way, you can measure your progress and celebrate small achievements along the way.

Embrace Mistakes and Failure:

Mistakes and failure are an inevitable part of life. No one is perfect, and everyone makes mistakes. Embracing mistakes and failure can help you overcome perfectionism by allowing you to see them as opportunities for growth and learning.

When you make a mistake or experience failure, take a step back and reflect on what went wrong. What can you learn from the experience? How can you use this knowledge to improve in the future? By reframing mistakes and failure as opportunities for growth, you can overcome the fear of making mistakes and embrace imperfection.

Practice Mindfulness:

Mindfulness is the practice of being present and fully engaged in the current moment. It involves paying attention to your thoughts, feelings, and surroundings without judgment.

Practicing mindfulness can help you overcome perfectionism by allowing you to become aware of your perfectionistic tendencies and observe them without judgment. When you notice yourself becoming overly critical or setting unrealistic standards, take a moment to breathe deeply and bring yourself back to the present moment.

Seek Support:

Overcoming perfectionism can be a challenging process, and it's important to seek support from friends, family, or a mental health professional. Talking about your struggles with someone who understands can help you feel less alone and more motivated to make positive changes.

Conclusion:

Perfectionism can be a source of stress, anxiety, and self-doubt. However, by recognizing and challenging your inner critic, practicing self-compassion, setting realistic goals, embracing mistakes and failure, practicing mindfulness, and seeking support, you can overcome perfectionism and embrace imperfection for greater happiness. Remember, you are enough just as you are, flaws and all. Embrace imperfection and unleash your inner joy.

35: The Art of Goal-Setting: Achieving Your Dreams and Finding Joy in the Journey

Introduction

When it comes to achieving happiness and fulfillment, one of the most important things we can do is set goals. Goals give us direction, motivation, and a sense of purpose. However, not all goals are created equal. In order to truly unleash your inner joy and achieve enduring happiness, you need to learn the art of goal-setting.

In this chapter, we will explore the science behind goal-setting and provide you with practical strategies to help you set and achieve your goals. We will also discuss how to find joy in the journey and avoid common pitfalls that can derail your progress. So let's get started!

The Science of Goal-Setting

Goal-setting is not just a feel-good activity – it is backed by science. Studies have shown that setting goals can increase motivation, improve performance, and boost well-being. In fact, a study published in the Journal of Applied Psychology found that people who set specific, challenging goals were more likely to achieve them and experience greater satisfaction with their lives.

So what makes a good goal? According to the well-known acronym SMART, goals should be Specific, Measurable, Achievable, Relevant, and Time-bound. Let's break down each of these components:

Specific: A specific goal is clear and well-defined. For example, "lose 10 pounds in 3 months" is a specific goal, whereas "lose weight" is not.

Measurable: A measurable goal has a way of tracking progress. In the example above, the ability to measure progress is built into the goal itself – the individual can weigh themselves and see if they are on track to lose 10 pounds in 3 months.

Achievable: An achievable goal is realistic and within reach. Setting a goal that is too lofty or impossible to achieve can lead to discouragement and failure.

Relevant: A relevant goal is aligned with your values and

priorities. For example, if your goal is to get in shape, but you hate exercise, it may not be a relevant goal for you.

Time-bound: A time-bound goal has a deadline attached to it. This helps to create a sense of urgency and can motivate you to take action.

Using the SMART framework can help you create goals that are well-defined, realistic, and motivating. However, there are other factors to consider when setting goals.

Strategies for Effective Goal-Setting

In addition to using the SMART framework, there are several other strategies you can use to set effective goals. Here are some of the most important ones:

Start with Your Why: Before you set a goal, it's important to understand why you want to achieve it. What is driving you? What are the underlying motivations behind your goal? Understanding your why can help you stay motivated and focused on your goal.

Break It Down: Large goals can be overwhelming, so it's important to break them down into smaller, manageable steps.

This can help you stay focused and make progress without feeling like you are facing an insurmountable task.

Visualize Success: Visualization is a powerful tool that can help you stay motivated and focused on your goal. Take some time each day to visualize yourself achieving your goal and experiencing the joy and fulfillment that comes with it.

Build a Support System: Achieving a goal is often easier when you have a support system in place. This can include friends, family, or a coach who can provide encouragement, accountability, and guidance along the way.

Be Flexible: It's important to be flexible and willing to adjust your goals as needed. Life is unpredictable, and circumstances may change. Being open to adjusting your goals can help you stay on track and avoid feeling discouraged by setbacks.

Finding Joy in the Journey

While achieving your goals is important, it's also important to find joy in the journey. Here are some strategies for finding joy in the process of working towards your goals:

35: THE ART OF GOAL-SETTING: ACHIEVING YOUR DREAMS AND FINDING JOY IN THE JOURNEY

Practice Gratitude: Taking time to appreciate the progress you've made and the things you have in your life can help you stay positive and motivated. Consider keeping a gratitude journal or taking a few minutes each day to reflect on the things you are thankful for.

Celebrate Small Wins: Achieving a big goal can take time, so it's important to celebrate small victories along the way. Whether it's hitting a milestone, completing a task, or receiving positive feedback, take time to acknowledge and celebrate your progress.

Embrace Failure: Failure is a natural part of the goal-setting process, and it's important to view it as a learning opportunity rather than a setback. When you experience setbacks or failures, take time to reflect on what you can learn from the experience and how you can use that knowledge to move forward.

Practice Self-Care: Taking care of your physical and mental well-being is essential for achieving your goals and finding joy in the journey. Make sure to prioritize things like getting enough sleep, eating healthy foods, and engaging in activities that bring you joy and relaxation.

35: THE ART OF GOAL-SETTING: ACHIEVING YOUR DREAMS AND FINDING JOY IN THE JOURNEY

Avoiding Common Pitfalls

Finally, there are several common pitfalls that can derail your progress towards achieving your goals. Here are some strategies for avoiding these pitfalls:

Avoid Overwhelm: Setting too many goals or taking on too much at once can lead to overwhelm and burnout. Focus on one or two goals at a time, and break them down into smaller, manageable steps.

Don't Compare Yourself to Others: Comparing your progress to others can be demotivating and lead to feelings of inadequacy. Remember that everyone's journey is unique, and focus on your own progress and growth.

Avoid Perfectionism: Striving for perfection can be a roadblock to progress and can lead to feelings of failure and inadequacy. Focus on progress rather than perfection, and celebrate small victories along the way.

Conclusion

Setting and achieving goals is an essential part of achieving lasting happiness and fulfillment. By using science-backed strategies like the SMART framework, visualization, and building a support system, you can set effective goals and work towards achieving them in a way that brings you joy and fulfillment. Remember to focus on the journey, celebrate small wins, and avoid common pitfalls like overwhelm, comparison, and perfectionism. With these strategies in mind, you can unleash your inner joy and achieve enduring happiness.

36: The Journey to Euphoria: Putting It All Together for Lasting Happiness

As human beings, we all strive for happiness. It's an innate desire, hard-wired into our DNA, and a goal that we all hope to achieve. However, what we often overlook is the fact that happiness is not something that can be achieved through external means alone. Rather, it's a state of mind that can only be achieved by cultivating the right mindset, and by making certain lifestyle changes that foster positivity, resilience, and a sense of inner peace.

In this chapter, we'll be taking a closer look at the journey to euphoria – the path that we must take to achieve enduring happiness. We'll be exploring some of the key science-backed strategies and mindset shifts that are crucial to this journey, as well as outlining some of the specific lifestyle changes that you can make to help you along the way.

But before we get started, it's important to note that the journey to euphoria is not a quick fix, nor is it something that can be achieved overnight. Rather, it's a process that requires time, effort, and dedication. It's a journey that will challenge you, push you out of your comfort zone, and force you to confront some of the limiting beliefs and negative thought patterns that may be holding you back from true happiness. But if you're willing to commit to this journey, to put in the work and to make the necessary changes, the rewards will be truly life-changing.

So, without further ado, let's dive in.

The first step on the journey to euphoria is to cultivate a growth mindset. This means shifting your perspective from one of fixed limitations to one of endless possibility. It's about embracing challenges, seeing failures as opportunities to learn and grow, and recognizing that your potential for success is not limited by your current circumstances or abilities.

To cultivate a growth mindset, it's important to start by challenging your own beliefs and assumptions about yourself and your abilities. Begin by identifying any negative self-talk or limiting beliefs that you may be holding onto, and work to replace them with more positive, empowering thoughts. For example, if you find yourself thinking, "I'm not good at this," try reframing that thought as, "I may not be good at this yet, but with practice and effort, I can improve."

Another key aspect of cultivating a growth mindset is to embrace failure as a natural part of the learning process. Instead of seeing failure as a reflection of your worth or abilities, see it as an opportunity to learn, grow, and improve. Recognize that every successful person has faced failure at some point in their journey, and that it's often these setbacks that ultimately lead to their greatest successes.

The next step on the journey to euphoria is to practice mindfulness. Mindfulness is the practice of being fully present in the moment, without judgment or distraction. It's about paying attention to your thoughts, emotions, and physical sensations, and learning to accept them without resistance or attachment.

To practice mindfulness, start by setting aside a few minutes each day to simply sit quietly and focus on your breath. You can do this by sitting in a comfortable position, closing your eyes, and bringing your attention to the sensation of your breath as it moves in and out of your body. When your mind inevitably starts to wander (as it will!), simply notice the distraction, and gently bring your attention back to your breath.

Over time, you can expand your mindfulness practice to include other activities, such as mindful eating, mindful movement (such as yoga or tai chi), or simply being fully present and engaged in your everyday tasks.

The third step on the journey to euphoria is to cultivate positive relationships. We are social beings, and our relationships with others play a critical role in our overall sense of well-being and happiness. To cultivate positive relationships, it's important to focus on building strong connections with those around us, including friends, family, and even colleagues.

One way to cultivate positive relationships is to practice empathy and active listening. This means taking the time to truly listen to others, and to try to understand their perspective and feelings. It also means being willing to put yourself in their shoes, and to show compassion and kindness towards them, even in difficult situations.

Another key aspect of cultivating positive relationships is to prioritize quality time with the people who matter most to you. This might mean scheduling regular date nights with your partner, setting aside time each week to catch up with a friend, or even simply taking the time to have a meaningful conversation with a coworker.

The fourth step on the journey to euphoria is to take care of your physical health. Our physical health is closely linked to our mental and emotional well-being, and making small lifestyle changes to improve our physical health can have a big impact on our overall happiness.

Some key strategies for improving physical health include getting regular exercise, eating a healthy diet, getting enough sleep, and managing stress. These might seem like simple changes, but they can have a powerful impact on your energy levels, mood, and overall sense of well-being.

The fifth and final step on the journey to euphoria is to practice gratitude. Gratitude is the practice of focusing on the good things in our lives, and taking the time to appreciate and express gratitude for them. By cultivating a sense of gratitude, we can shift our focus away from negativity and scarcity, and towards positivity and abundance.

36: THE JOURNEY TO EUPHORIA: PUTTING IT ALL TO-GETHER FOR LASTING HAPPINESS

To practice gratitude, try starting each day by writing down three things you're grateful for. These might be big things (like your health, your family, or your career), or small things (like a warm cup of coffee, a beautiful sunset, or a kind word from a friend). By making gratitude a daily habit, you can begin to retrain your brain to focus on the positive aspects of your life, rather than getting bogged down by the negatives.

Putting It All Together

So, there you have it – the five key steps on the journey to euphoria. By cultivating a growth mindset, practicing mindfulness, cultivating positive relationships, taking care of your physical health, and practicing gratitude, you can begin to shift your mindset and your lifestyle in a way that promotes lasting happiness and fulfillment.

Of course, these steps are not a one-size-fits-all solution – everyone's journey to euphoria will look different, and the strategies that work best for one person may not work as well for another. But by starting with these key principles, and by experimenting with different strategies and mindset shifts, you can begin to uncover the unique path to happiness that is right for you.

So, whether you're just starting out on your journey to euphoria, or you've been on this path for a while, remember to
be patient, be kind to yourself, and stay committed to the
process. With time, effort, and dedication, you can achieve
enduring happiness and unleash your inner joy – and that is
truly something worth striving for.

Thank You

As we reach the end of this book, I want to say thanks for reading this book.

I want to get this information out to as many people as possible. If you found this book helpful, I would greatly appreciate you leaving me a review. This helps others find the book as well.

Disclaimer

This document is geared towards providing exact and reliable information in regards to the topic and issue covered. The publication is sold on the idea that the publisher is not required to render an accounting, officially permitted, or otherwise, qualified services. If advice is necessary, legal, financial, medical or professional, a practiced individual in the profession should be ordered.

This information is not presented by a financial or medical practitioner and is for entertainment, educational and informational purposes only. The content is not intended as a substitute for professional medical advice, diagnosis, or treatment. Always seek the advice of your physician or other qualified health care provider with any questions you may have regarding a medical condition. Never disregard professional medical advice or delay in seeking it because of something you have read.

The information provided herein is stated to be truthful and consistent, in that any liability, in terms of inattention or otherwise, by any usage or abuse of any policies, processes, or directions contained within is the solitary and utter responsibility of the recipient reader. Under no circumstances

DISCLAIMER

will any legal responsibility or blame be held against the publisher for any reparation, damages, or monetary loss due to the information herein, either directly or indirectly.

www.ingramcontent.com/pod-product-compliance
Lightning Source LLC
Chambersburg PA
CBHW060506130626
46553CB00002B/421